LONGHORN COWBOY

THE WESTERN FRONTIER LIBRARY

Longhorn Cowboy

By
James H. Cook

Edited by Howard R. Driggs
With a Foreword by Donald E. Worcester
Drawings by Herbert Stoops

UNIVERSITY OF OKLAHOMA PRESS

NORMAN

By James H. Cook

Fifty Years on the Old Frontier (New Haven, 1923; Norman, 1957, 1980)
Longhorn Cowboy (New York, 1942; Norman, 1984)

Cook, James H. (James Henry), 1857-1942.
 Longhorn cowboy.

 (The Western frontier library; 55)
 1. Cook, James H. (James Henry), 1857-1942. 2. Cowboys—West (U.S.)—Biography. 3. Cowboys—Texas—Biography. 4. West (U.S.)—Biography. 5. Texas—Biography. 6. Ranch life—West (U.S.) 7. Ranch life—Texas. 8. Cattle trade—West (U.S.) 9. Cattle trade—Texas. 10. West (U.S.)—Social life and customs. 11. Texas—Social life and customs. I. Driggs, Howard R. (Howard Roscoe), 1873- II. Title. III. Series.
F596.C74   1984   976.4'06'0924   84-7283
ISBN 0-8061-1877-6

Copyright © 1942 by James H. Cook and Howard R. Driggs. New edition copyright © 1984 by the University of Oklahoma Press, Norman, Publishing Division of the University. Manufactured in the U.S.A. First printing of the new edition.

The paper in this book meets the guidelines for permanence and durability of the Committee on Production Guidelines for Book Longevity of the Council on Library Resources, Inc.

CONTENTS

FOREWORD	ix
I : FRONTIER BOYHOOD	1
II : CABIN BOY	8
III : CHISHOLM TRAIL	14
IV : SHORTHORN COWBOY	26
V : RAWHIDE	33
VI : BRUSH POPPER	44
VII : WILD CATTLE RANGE	53
VIII : BRONCHO BUSTING	62
IX : MEXICAN VAQUEROS	70
X : GUNS AND GAME	79
XI : OUTLAWS AND REDSKINS	88
XII : LONGHORNS NORTHWARD	97

XIII : START–AND STAMPEDE!	105
XIV : COMANCHES	117
XV : TRICKS AND TROUBLES	129
XVI : MUSTANGS	141
XVII : CAPORAL MAC	153
XVIII : TRAIL ADVENTURES	167
XIX : SIOUX PARLEY	180
XX : BIG GAME	189
XXI : HUNTER'S LUCK	200
XXII : APACHE OUTBREAK	207
XXIII : GERONIMO'S TRAIL	221
XXIV : HOME ON THE RANGE	230

ILLUSTRATIONS

Mrs. Kills Above and James H. Cook	viii
Our job was to ride slowly around the herds to see that none strayed or were driven off by Indians.	16-17
The infuriated animal charged in the direction of Mr. Slaughter and me.	36-37
These inconsiderate callers had the unneighborly intention of ambushing us.	92-93
Taking those great herds to market was a serious business involving large sums, and was in no wise a Wild West show.	108-109
Not daring to rise up to a proper shooting position, I took a pot shot at him as he passed.	126-127
As I whirled my horse, the lurking redskin drove a dogwood arrow into my leg.	138-139
Trying to appear greatly pleased at meeting him, I said, "How, *mita kola*."	186-187
Geronimo's rear guard concealed themselves on a bluff which could not be scaled by troops, and fired into the command.	216-217

Mrs. Kills Above, the last child of Chief Red Cloud of the Oglala Sioux, and James H. Cook. From a photograph taken at Agate, Nebraska, in August, 1937, by Mr. Floyd McCaffree of Scottsbluff, Nebraska.

FOREWORD

by Donald E. Worcester

Unlike his seafaring father, who spent his life on the quarterdeck of a sailing vessel, James Henry Cook preferred life in the saddle. Raised by a pioneer family in Michigan after the death of his mother, he became an expert marksman with the rifle. After one cruise as a cabin boy, he and a companion traveled by railroad and river steamboat to Leavenworth, Kansas, in search of adventure. There in 1872, the fifteen-year-old youth was hired to herd Texas cattle near Fort Harker, three miles east of Leavenworth. Later he joined some cowboys returning to Texas.

After reaching San Antonio, Cook signed on with cowman Ben Slaughter, whose ranch was south of town near the Frio River. Slaughter sent him with a group of Mexican and Indian vaqueros under John Longworth to catch wild cattle in the *brasada*, or brush country, between the Nueces River and the Rio Grande. Mesquite, cactus and a rich variety of thorny shrubs made the brush country almost impenetrable without heavy protective clothing. Called brushpoppers, the men were a little-known kind of cowboy because few literate Anglos cared to engage in the dangerous and unglamorous work.

Brushpopping was very different from handling cattle on the open range, and Cook's description of life in the *brasada* is a rare and priceless bit of frontier lore. Cowboys who tried brushpopping without proper clothing pulled thorns from their arms and legs for weeks, and usually they vowed never to go near the brush country again. On the other hand, some men who spent their lives in the brush were afraid to venture out onto the treeless plains.

Brushpoppers lived in isolation for months at a time, daily pulling thorns from their flesh with the point of a knife blade and doctoring their wounds and ailments with simple but effective folk remedies. The vaqueros, who were so skillful with rawhide riatas that they even fought duels with them, willingly taught Cook their skills.

The brush country was the refuge of outlaws because few lawmen cared to hunt wanted men in the inhospitable land. Only occasionally did cavalry troops or Texas Rangers enter it on the trail of horse thieves or cattle rustlers. Ranchers and cowboys refused to help them, for it was perilous to incur the wrath of the desperadoes. More dangerous to brushpoppers were the bands of Comanches and Lipan Apaches who occasionally attacked the vaqueros. Tarantulas, scorpions, centipedes, ticks, lice, and rattlesnakes also found the region congenial. Brushpoppers adopted the Indian practice of placing vermin-infested clothing on anthills and allowing the ants to carry off the pests.

After he had become expert in handling the mustang cow ponies and wild longhorns, Cook was eager to accompany a herd of cattle up the trail to Kansas. He applied to Joe Roberts, who was trail boss for the first of several Slaughter herds to start north during that season. Roberts, who knew Cook could handle cattle as well as his Henry rifle, replied, "If you can ride for the next four months without a whole night's sleep, and turn your gun loose on any damned Injun that tries to get our horses, well, get ready."

In the early days of trailing, as Cook informs us, it was customary for cowmen to take every suitable steer that their cowboys gathered, regardless of brand. Honest men kept records of the various strays, deducted their expenses from the sale price, and reimbursed the owners. This was a most satisfactory arrangement for owners of strayed steers. But when too many drovers proved forgetful of their obligations, inspectors were appointed to record the number of cattle of each brand in every trail herd. They kept lists on file at county courthouses.

Roberts's crew for managing 2,500 steers consisted of twelve cowboys and a cook, who was next in importance to the trail boss. The cook, more than anyone else, could make life bearable for the trail hands by providing hot, tasty meals in any kind of weather. He also served as doctor and nurse, with a few simple medicines and cloth for bandages. At roundup time and on the trail the chuck wagon was home and headquarters, and the cook was its monarch. Only a fool argued with a trail cook.

Cowboys on the trail faced a variety of dangers and hardships, and Cook experienced everything the trail had to offer. Comanches attacked them one night and drove off some of their horses. Cook and several others followed the Indians for twenty miles, surprised their camp, and recovered their horses, along with fifteen Comanche ponies. At other times the cowboys were not so fortunate and lost all of their extra horses.

Cook also learned firsthand about stampedes by unintentionally causing one. A cow had bedded down away from the herd, and out of curiosity Cook wanted to see how close he could pass by her when riding around the herd on night guard. Finally he rode close enough to touch her with his foot, and the stampede was on. The next day two hundred steers could not be found.

During that season every river from the Red to the Arkansas was "big swimming," that is, at flood stage. Thunder- and hailstorms and sleeping on soggy ground, or going without sleep for several days at a time, were among the joys of the trail. When the ground was covered with water, three exhausted men would form a triangle, each resting his head on the ankles of another. When all else failed, Cook put tobacco juice on his eyelids to keep awake—a method he did not recommend highly.

He found the cowboys admirable. "No painting or word picture of the life of the early cowboy has represented, nor could it represent, many of the hardships and dangers which attended those who constantly, day and night, rode with the herd," Cook wrote. "Their chief shelter was their own weatherbeaten skins. Yet despite all rigors of the trail and its many dangers, these heroic men were marked by loyalty to their work. They stayed with the herd, despite all hazards."

In Cook's day there were still thousands of mustangs roaming the plains. They lured tame animals away from camps, and the tame ones became wilder and warier than the mustangs. Renegade mules were the "most wisely wild creatures imaginable," Cook tells us. When mules were with mustangs, those bands were almost impossible to catch, for the mules were keenly alert to any sign of danger. Cook describes the methods mustangers used to catch the wild horses, including "creasing." Supposedly, a bullet striking a mustang's neck at the crest would stun it long enough for a man to tie its legs. Cook tried it once, but like most others who admitted making the experiment, to his deep chagrin he killed a splendid wild stallion.

On one of Cook's trips up the trail a tornado struck about the time the herd reached the Canadian River. Violent gusts of wind and heavy hailstones scattered the cattle and horses, battered and bruised the cowboys, and covered the ground with water and ice. They had hastily staked down the chuck wagon, but it was torn from its moorings and overturned. They found the cattle (which had given some Cheyenne Indians a bit of additional excitement by stampeding through their camp) safe and uninjured after the storm had passed.

In Wyoming, after his fifth trip up the trail, Cook quit trailing and teamed up with Wild Horse Charlie Alexander, a famous mustanger, to supply deer and antelope meat for the town of Cheyenne and the Union Pacific Railroad. Cook also conducted hunting parties for English sportsmen. These occupations proved more profitable than trailing cattle, and he soon accumulated $10,000. In 1882 he helped Harold C. Wilson, one of his English friends, establish the WS ranch near Silver City, New Mexico. In partnership with Wilson, Cook was managing the WS during Geronimo's last outbreak, when Apaches raided several ranches in the area.

In 1886, Cook returned to Cheyenne to marry Kate Graham. She considered New Mexico a violent land, and so he sold his interest in the WS ranch and bought her father's 04 ranch on the Niobara River in northwestern Nebraska, where he raised cattle and trotting horses. He became well acquainted with Sioux chief Red Cloud at Pine Ridge, across the South Dakota border, and the chief and his people frequently visited the 04. During the Ghost Dance outbreak of 1890–91, Cook was called to Pine Ridge to serve with the army scouts, and he was there when the massacre occurred at Wounded Knee Creek.

On the 04, Cook discovered the Agate Springs Fossil Quarry, which has been called "the most remarkable deposit of mammalian remains of Tertiary Age that has ever been found in any part of the world." Many eastern scientists visited the ranch to collect fossils, and in 1965 it became the Agate Fossil Beds National Monument. Cook's son Harold, named after his English partner, was well acquainted with visiting scientists. As a result of their encouragement, he became a well-known paleontologist.

Before writing *Longhorn Cowboy*, Cook wrote *Fifty Years on the Old Frontier* (Yale University Press, 1923; University of Oklahoma Press, 1957), which remains one of the classics of the old West. In *Longhorn Cowboy*, Cook recounts his youthful experiences, as well as some episodes he had not detailed in his earlier work. The Cook story was filled in and extended by his son, Harold J. Cook, in *Tales of the 04 Ranch* (University of Nebraska Press, 1968). Together these books are a remarkable trilogy of western Americana.

I : FRONTIER BOYHOOD

In 1859, when I was two, my mother died. My father, a descendant of the famous English navigator, Captain Cook, wanted to continue the life he loved as captain of a clipper, and he found me a home with a pioneer Michigan family. Father was a typical old-time sailor, who had no desire for any home but his ship. I never lived with him, so I knew him only through others. I remember that one of his commands was the four-decked man-'o-war *Asia,* later used as a training ship in the harbor at Portsmouth, England.

My new home with Edward Prosper Titus was one where industry and frugality were practiced, and Christian precepts and virtues strictly observed. The Tituses were a type of solid American pioneer that commanded respect. In their estimation there was nothing more important in life than to prepare themselves and those in their keeping for the life to come; and it is to the loving care of this family that I am indebted for a wholesome training which stood me in good stead in the later rough days on the wild cattle trails of the old West.

Mrs. Titus made my homespun clothing, knitted my socks, and made the scarfs that kept my neck protected. She prepared dyes to give color to the various garments she made.

Mr. Titus was an expert carpenter, and like other skilled mechanics, he liked sharp tools to work with. Being a strong man, he failed to realize that I was not, and quite frequently called upon me to turn the grindstone. Round and round that old-fashioned stone had to go, with my small arms propelling it. Sometimes it took hours to sharpen the tools to his liking. How well I remember that old grindstone!

Sometimes the family would go in the wagon out to Mrs. Titus' father's farm, about five miles from our home. I liked to visit Grandfather Wells, but I preferred to walk through the forest to his farm — the oxen were too slow for an impatient youngster.

It was at Grandpa Well's home that I had my first experience firing a gun. One morning I was permitted to accompany the men on a hunting trip. As they returned, I proudly carried one of the squirrels they had killed. It was impossible not to see how happy I was to be allowed to have even this small share in the proceedings. One of the men asked, good-naturedly, "Like to fire a shot, son?"

They might as well have asked me whether I wanted a million dollars. The old musket was loaded with buckshot and handed to me, and I was told to kneel down behind a shaving horse and shoot at an ash barrel about twenty-five feet away.

The men were full of advice.

"The stock's too long for the little feller to reach the trigger. He'd best put it under his arm."

"Aim careful, son."

And, chuckling, "Can't you pull the trigger, Jim? Take two fingers to it."

Earnestly I followed directions, aimed slowly, and with care — and got results. The kick of the gun upset me, and gave the men a good laugh; but I had pleasure too, for I hit the barrel with about four buckshot.

My schooldays I spent in the old Union School. That I was considered by some to be bright in my school work was, I admit, due not so much to any unusual brilliancy on my part as it was to the unflagging attention I was required to give to my lessons. One day at Sabbath school I rather startled my teachers by having fourteen verses of the Bible committed to memory; the truth is I had pored over the verses under the uncompromising and patient eyes of Mrs. Titus, who, having been a school ma'am in her younger days, knew how to handle small boys. I fear this religious atmosphere in which I lived while I remained in the

Titus home was unnatural to a boy of my spirit, yet I believe I was better for it.

I was nine when I left the Tituses and went to work in a foundry and machine shop in Comstock, four miles from Kalamazoo. There I was the happy engineer of a big, noisy, iron tank called a "rattler," which scoured the various small castings made in the shop, to rid them of sand and partly to polish them. My earsplitting machine and I were banished to the basement, where the risk of deafness to other employees and visitors was lessened.

In Comstock I met the man to whom I am indebted for the training that helped me through the after years on the frontier — Alden Brown, expert gunsmith. He could make a rifle, lock, stock, and barrel. He was especially skillful in making the Kentucky squirrel rifles then in common use.

Alden Brown was a big man with graying hair and stooped shoulders, and quite deaf. He appealed to me as being the most wonderful man I had ever met. Whenever I could get a chance I was at his shop; and I fear those chances were more frequent than my work should have allowed.

Because of my interest in his work, he became interested in me, and took me along on his shorter hunting, fishing, and trapping expeditions, on which no other boy was ever allowed to accompany him and his sons. With him I learned how to paddle and pole a canoe, to catch fish, to use a rifle, to observe wild life, and to do many other things that were invaluable to me later.

One evening Mr. Brown invited me to go with him in his canoe to try to spear fish. He placed me at one end of the canoe to pole through the water of the bayou while he attended to the jack-light, which was made by setting pitch-wood alight in an iron basket on the end of a bar jutting out from the bow of the canoe. The light would both attract and blind the fish, so that an expert with a spear could easily secure them.

I shoved off, while he stood erect in the bow, ready for action. Just as we left the bank, I saw him lunge with the spear — a fine implement with five prongs at the end of a ten-foot handle. A fish had darted under the canoe and come out on the other side like a streak. I saw the spear wobble furiously. Swinging the boat toward it, he grabbed the spear handle, not too tightly, but just letting it continue to wobble a little.

"Ha-ha, Jimmy," he exclaimed; "we've got him."

After what seemed an age the fish was lifted into the boat — the largest pickerel I had ever seen, weighing about sixteen pounds.

"Well, Jimmy," said Mr. Brown, "I think that's all the fish we want." And he proceeded to knock the remaining wood out of the jackpot, lock the canoe to a tree on the bank, and take the big pickerel home.

There were hordes of gray, black, and red squirrels in the Michigan forests, where their principal food — walnuts, butternuts, hazelnuts, and hickory nuts — grew in great abundance. To get a shot at one of the wise little fellows was not easy, for they managed to keep a tree between themselves and the hunter. By concealing himself and throwing a stone to the other side of the tree, the hunter might cause the squirrel to run around and look about. Given such an opportunity for a few seconds, the hunter might get his game. Usually two hunted together, one to use the gun while the other attempted to bring the squirrels to the side of the tree where the hunter could get a shot.

Alden Brown trained me not only in woodcraft and hunting, but he also gave me the rare privilege of testing his rifles, preferring my younger eyes and steadier nerves to his own. He would take a patch of white cloth about an inch square and tack it securely on the side of a tree. I would lie down behind a log thirty or forty feet away, placing on it some moss on which to rest the muzzle, and fire four shots at the target. If I could shoot that white patch out with the four shots, he considered the gun finished. Mr. Brown trained me to take perfect care of a gun. After each shot the rifle was wiped out. He instructed me always to pull the trigger with gentle pressure — never to jerk it when firing. He remarked on a characteristic which is still with me, of keeping both eyes open in aiming.

This pioneer gunsmith gave me during my boyhood such training as helped me all through my life. Certainly his influence did much to start me off on a career different from what any of my boyhood companions grew up to.

I enjoyed many diversions in Comstock. I coasted in winter and skated on a pair of Holland skates with thick wooden soles and runners which curved over the toe. I often went berrying, too, usually devouring my berries on the spot.

I never allowed myself to be imposed upon. I had a great many freckles which often occasioned such a remark as, "When did the devil throw bran in your face?" This always roused my ire, and caused a good many fights. I felt called upon, too, to defend my smaller brother Jack.

One day I stood with my little spear in hand, watching the blacksmith at work, when the town bully, bigger and older than I, suddenly seized my spear and threw it across the shop, saying, "That thing's no good."

As he came toward me I grabbed a buggy wheel spoke which lay on a workbench near me, and jabbed it into the pit of his stomach, which jerked his hands down, and then I followed through with a whack on his head which floored him. No doubt this caused him to see stars, and as soon as he could get on his feet he started home, probably inventing on his way an excuse for the big lump on his head. That shillalah must have caused him to postpone the date for my trouncing, which he never did undertake.

II : CABIN BOY

While I lived with the Thomsons I was a guest many times at the home of an aristocratic Irishman by the name of Sandes, whose son, Charlie, and nephew, Rafe Sandes, owned and sailed a schooner in the lumber trade on Lake Michigan.

Rafe and Charlie seemed to like me — probably because I was a good listener. They told me that if I ever wanted to become a sailor, I could join their ship. Charlie was captain, and Rafe, the owner, always accompanied him on the schooner's trips.

Probably I had some of my father's love for the sea, for I decided that it would be a fine thing to take advantage of the Sandes' offer. I made arrangements to be taken on as cabin boy, packed my grip — a small undertaking — and joined ship at St. Joseph, at the mouth of the Kalamazoo River.

It was the spring of the year, and the ice had just gone out. After the ship had been loaded with lumber, a tug was engaged to tow us out of the river. There was what seemed to me to be a terrible storm raging. Despite the warning flag flying from the government signal station, we pulled out into the storm — a risky business, for the insurance would be forfeited if the vessel were lost.

Rafe, being drunk, insisted on taking the wheel, and throwing it hard, first up, then down, causing the schooner to make strange patterns through the heavy gale.

"Either steady that wheel or we'll cut the towline," the tug warned at last.

Rafe paid not the slightest attention to a little matter such as that, and the tug carried out its threat. We were on our own, and being tossed about dangerously on the open lake.

As we plunged and bucked about in the heavy sea, one of the crew — Aleck, an old-time, deep-sea sailor — jumped into the wheel pit, grabbed Rafe by the shoulders, and flung him from the wheel.

"Stay there," he ordered. "My life is worth as much to me as yours is to you."

The schooner was now being buffeted about so that it was impossible for Aleck to hold the helm alone. He called for help, and another seaman leaped into the pit, grabbed one side of the wheel, and shouted, "Blow, God! There's a man at the wheel!"

With my Sabbath school training fresh in mind, I was sure that no ship could last a moment with such a man aboard; surely, I thought, God would accept this challenge and blow us out of existence. I was most unhappy, humped up in the wheel pit, holding to a life line, and expecting to go to Davy Jones's locker with every lurch of the ship. But the two sailors regained control of the ship, and we rode out the storm.

In my own mind I believed I was aboard to learn something about sailing, but no doubt the crew thought I was there to get underfoot. Their work was no child's play. They had to know how to handle lumber green from the saw, as well as to perform the regular duties of able seamen. When a gale came up, Captain Sandes would give orders from the quarterdeck to the mate, who repeated them directly to the men. In heavy storms, sail had to be shortened, and the headsails reefed and the topsails taken down.

If I didn't earn my salt by my work, I at least provided amusement for all. One day Rafe, standing near me when the topsails were being shifted, sang out, "Jim, lay aloft, and shift those fore gaff topsail halyards."

We were coming about in order to take advantage of the wind. To obey my orders meant some risky climbing; but I was going to be a sailor, so I thought, "Here goes!" and running to the first shrouds, I started aloft on the mainmast to the crosstrees, a long way from the fore gaff topsail where I was to do my work. When I reached the crosstrees on the mainmast and hesitated to consider my next move, Sandes shouted, "Lay across up there on the triatic stay!"

Between the masts of the schooner, which were thirty or forty feet apart, a large cable was stretched to steady the masts in the pitch of the ship. It was by means of this cable that I was to reach the spot where my work was to be done.

Believing that this was a part of a sailor's regular duty, I got hold of the stay, or guyline, and started across hand over hand, with my body hanging. Old Aleck saw me from the deck.

"You idiot," he roared, "get back there to the mainmast!"

I was about ten feet out from the mainmast. When I returned to the crosstrees and came down on deck, the men had a good laugh at what was, to them, my foolhardy adventure, and I began to see in the feat a certain danger which hadn't been apparent to me when I was carrying out my orders. Of course, while I was performing my acrobatic stunts in mid air the halyards had been shifted by a seaman.

Another time I had started aloft and was about halfway to the crosstrees when I put my hand on a bat that had made fast to the shroud, probably at some lumber port. Scared out of all thinking by its squeals, I let go my hold. My wits returned just in time for me to grab a rope and save myself from a plunge into Lake Michigan from which I might never have been rescued. The ship was heeled over before the wind, and scudding along.

Not everything that happened to me aboard the Sandes schooner was dangerous or thrilling, but I saw and did many things that were interesting. I saw my first mirage aboard that ship. Approaching the port of Chicago one day, before the city could be seen, I happened to look up into the sky, and saw the city there, upside down. I was impressed.

"Look," I exclaimed, pointing. "What's that?"

The men were indifferent. "Haven't you ever seen a mirage before?" someone asked.

Altogether, I enjoyed my stay aboard the Sandes ship, and certainly I was responsible for a good many laughs that the men enjoyed. I ended my cabin-boy days as impulsively and suddenly as I had begun them, by running away. I slipped ashore one day when we were in the port of Chicago, and hid in a lumber pile until I saw the schooner sail away.

As the loneliness of my situation dawned on me, I was having a good crying spell when a policeman discovered me. I told him I was alone, and that I had only a little money.

"Come along with me," he said, "and I'll show you a sailors' boarding house where you can stop and think up the best thing to do."

Though I did go with him, I didn't stay long in that house, for it was an unpleasant place, tenanted by rough, drunken sailors. Remembering a young friend who lived with relatives in a town in Indiana not far distant, I secured passage on a train and went to him. Pete Smith and his folks treated me very kindly, but I stayed only a short time. Pete and I got our young heads together and decided to try our fortunes elsewhere. Pete didn't require much persuasion, for his foster father's truck garden wasn't what Pete considered a worthy field for his talents; and I was always ready enough for new adventures.

III : CHISHOLM TRAIL

Pete and I headed west. The railroad took us as far as St. Joseph on the Missouri, and we went by steamboat down the river to Leavenworth, Kansas. In a little hotel in Leavenworth we met some cattlemen who had a problem that interested us.

They had contracted with the government to supply beef to soldier posts in the region of Fort Harker, near Ellsworth, Kansas. Since their big herds were often held to graze on the good land near Fort Harker, cowhands were needed to guard the cattle until they were distributed in small lots to the various posts.

Fort Harker was a rough place. Cowhands in charge of the herds were inclined to pay more attention to drinking and gambling than to the cattle left to their care. The cattlemen, disgusted, were looking for some younger men who had not acquired bad habits, and advised us to go at once to Fort Harker.

Thus we became herders of a bunch of Texas longhorns. Our pay was twenty-five dollars a month, and we were furnished with tent, provisions, saddle horses, and saddles. Our work was simply to ride slowly around the herds as they grazed, watching to see that none strayed or were driven off by Indians. Although there were still buffalo to be had, the Indians had by this time acquired a preference for the taste of beef. Then too, running off cattle saved them the trouble of chasing wild buffalo, and the risk of coming into contact with other Indians with whom they were not on friendly terms.

We must have been moderately good cow herders, for our employers kept us on until they finally disposed of the big herd. Pete, meantime, had become interested in Kansas soil and the Kansas pioneers, and he persuaded his Indiana relatives to come out to Ellsworth to settle. We were good pals, but our trails parted when the herding near Fort Harker ended.

At the time when this work was coming to an end, I happened to meet some Texas cowboys who had just made a trip with cattle up the old Chisholm Trail. This historic route was originally a wagon road made by Jesse Chisholm, grandson of the last chief of the Cherokees, who used bull teams to freight government supplies from Leavenworth to military posts in Texas. Later he drove longhorns over his old wagon road, which in time became the most famous of all the

Our job was to ride slowly around the herds to see that none strayed or were driven off by Indians.

Texas cattle trails.[1] Cattle by the thousands, gathered from the ranges of Texas, kept this famed route smoking with dust during the years immediately following the Civil War.

The Texas cowhands had had many exciting experiences on their drive northward along the Chisholm Trail. Indians had twice attempted to steal the herd of horses from which the cowboys selected their fresh mounts each day. The first attempt was made by night, and all but the horses of the night herders and the ponies hobbled or picketed near the camp were driven off.

Leaving most of the cowboys to hold the herd, three of the men set out to recapture the horses. After riding hard for two full days, swimming rivers, and going without food for twenty-four hours, they overtook the red raiders, who had relaxed their vigilance, feeling that they were far enough away from the scene of the raid to be safe.

In the darkness the three cowboys crept up on the Indians and opened the fight, killing one Indian and wounding several others before the redskins were aware that they had been overtaken. There were about twelve savages in the band; they sent a few arrows in the direction of the shots, and some more into the bunch of horses, and then fled on their Indian ponies toward their Comanche camp, without the horses which they had probably

---

[1] The Chisholm Trail has often been confused with the Chis'um Trail, running northwest out of Texas to Pueblo, Colorado. The Chisholm Trail went northward to Kansas.

intended to sell or trade to drivers starting up the trail from the South.

The shots roused the horses and caused them to scatter, but before they could run far the men rounded them up and headed back for camp. The rest of the outfit had given up the three for dead when they rode in, hungry as wolves, and with their clothes soaked from frequent swimming.

The next time the Comanches attempted to steal the horses, the cowboys were ready for them. Disappointed, the Indians in retaliation fired into the cattle, causing a stampede which took all hands to control, and during which five hundred head were lost. Most of these missing longhorns, however, were later brought in by another trail outfit, and the owner was notified. Such square dealing often was encountered on the trail, although more frequently missing cattle were not recovered.

Despite such stories of dangers — or maybe because of them — I decided to join the Texas cowboys for the trip down the Chisholm Trail. I had money enough from my cattle herding to buy what was needed for the long ride. A good little Comanche pony cost me fifteen dollars, and I got a fine second-hand Texas saddle for five dollars. Cowboy equipment was cheap; often the saddle-weary Texas cowboys sold their equipment at the end of the northward journey, preferring for a change to travel back to Texas in the "varnished cars."

Another thing I bought was a long-barreled, heavy, muzzle-loading rifle, made by Hawkins of St. Louis. I soon found out that this was not a handy saddle gun, and a good grade of powder could not easily be obtained for it. I acquired a breech-loading Spencer in its place as soon as I could, and this proved to be a real "humdinger"; the person using it often could hear its bullet hum as it whirled end-over-end through the air. But I soon condemned this gun too, because of the large caliber, heavy bullet it took, and the light charge of low-grade powder used in the cartridges. It was essential that we have good weapons on the cattle trails.

The cowboy's horse, too, was a highly important part of his equipment, and his performance on his mount was his badge of trade. In those days a man needed skill in both riding and shooting in order to keep his seat on a broncho and his head on his shoulders. Almost anyone could buy an outfit, from sombrero to spurs, but if he failed to keep his seat on a good cow horse in action, he didn't remain a cowboy long; his bones might soon be bleaching in the brush.

It was late in June when we started for San Antonio. The life of the trail moved about us as we rode leisurely southward. Game abounded; thousands of deer and turkeys ranged the blackjack oak country; great herds of buffalo and bands of antelope were seen on the more open plains. In the Indian Territory, flocks of passenger pigeons, the last I ever saw that I could be certain of, were flying through the timber. We killed what game we needed to supplement the salt pork, coffee, flour, and other supplies carried by our pack horses.

At night we camped in the open, and after supper simply curled up on the ground and went to sleep — the pneumatic mattress was not in style at that particular time. A "Tucson bed" was quite a common thing on that trip, and on many a trip thereafter. For those who may not understand, I will explain that the Tucson bed is made by lying on your stomach and covering that with your back. It was allowable to put your saddle and saddle blanket over your head, should you happen to have such articles with you, as protection from any hailstones larger than hens' eggs.

Unless there was danger from Indians, only one or two of the horses were picketed, and the rest hobbled; a horse made fast to a pin through the night had little opportunity to get food. On this trip most of our animals were hobbled, for the Indians we saw did not bother us, perhaps because they could see that we were cowboys going down the trail after more cattle herds from which they could later exact toll.

The Indians of that region had adopted at least one expression of the white man — "wo-haw." This they picked up from bullwhackers who were constantly using it with their teams. When an Indian rode up to a cow herder going north and said "You-me wo-haw," he meant, "You give me a beef." Some tribes were even more emphatic in their demands.

Almost the only white men to be seen in the Indian Territory except for government employees at military posts were either whisky peddlers or United States marshals in pursuit of them. Indians supplied with "firewater" became crazed to the point of being quarrelsome and dangerous; a great many Indian troubles in the West were caused by liquor. The red men were so wild to get it that they would trade horses, furs, and other things so valuable to traders that they took great risks in the dangerous game. The government tried, by inflicting severest penalties, to stop whisky peddling among the tribes. The penalty was in most cases death. A number of peddlers were hanged at Fort Smith, Arkansas, the judges there being ready to dispose of such lawbreakers without delay.

We crossed the boundary between Indian Territory and Texas at the Red River ford on the old stage route. It was a big stream, and we had to swim our horses. A shack or two were the last evidences of the site of the stage station, and I am told that these were later blown away in a tornado.

On the Texas side we entered a country covered with blackjack oak, through which we traveled until we reached San Antonio, avoiding towns in order to find good feed for our horses.

Even at that time San Antonio was a city,

though not a very large one. The old Plaza Militaire, Plaza Major, and the Menger Hotel were show places. The Green Front and Jack Harris theaters, or variety shows, were in full blast, as were all the gambling places. Attractive houses built of adobe fronted the San Antonio River. Ancient Spanish missions encroached upon the old city. The historic Alamo stood partly demolished by the artillery fire of the fight that raged there while Texans battled for their freedom. It was a new world to me, and intensely interesting. We camped outside town, where we could find grass, up toward the storied San Pedro Springs.

Frontiersmen had much in common, and established acquaintance readily. In San Antonio folks from far and wide got together in a friendly way; one could approach another and without saying "I beg your pardon," start a conversation. All the old-timers I met appeared to take a tolerant interest in any youngster who saw fit to talk to them. By that time I considered myself so much of an old-timer that I doubtless tried to assume a poker face and pretend not to be interested in anything. But I kept eyes and ears open to receive what impressions this new country offered.

Soon after my arrival in San Antonio I was fortunate enough to meet one of the most noted frontiersmen of Texas — Captain "Bigfoot" Wallace. He told me the history of the fight at the Alamo. When he recounted how that little band of fearless men died, fighting against about as long odds as the greatest warriors of earth could desire, the brave old veteran became fired with enthusiasm; and certainly he got me excited to the point of thinking that those heroes of the Alamo were the greatest men that ever lived, except, perhaps, Ethan Allen or Daniel Boone.

This strapping giant had come from his native Virginia to Texas in 1836, just after the battle of San Jacinto. In 1842 he fought in the battle of Salado. Later, with the Mier expedition, he and other Texans were captured by Mexicans, and went through some man-testing experiences. Wallace told of the time when he and others were lined up, blindfolded, and given an opportunity to decide their fate. A jar partly filled with beans, one-tenth of which were black, was placed before them, and each man was required to thrust in a hand and draw out a bean. If it was white, his life was spared; if black, he was led out pronto and shot. Bigfoot, and Ben Slaughter, who later became my employer, were fortunate enough to get hold of white beans. It is possible that Bigfoot, being a great joker and popular with his captors, may have been helped a bit by the guards.

Though his life was spared, Wallace's freedom was withheld until some years later when our government interceded and obtained his release. He returned to Texas, which remembers him today as one of its most picturesque pioneers. For some years he drove an overland stage; during the latter part of his stage-driving career he had charge of the route from San Antonio to El Paso, one of the most dangerous stretches on the whole line.

When I met Captain Wallace he had retired from this work to his horse ranch out on Atascosa Creek, where he was trying to breed high-class saddle horses from Steeldust and Copperbottom stock. About a year later he gave me one of the best of his three-year-old colts.

Wallace deserved his reputation for running down marauding Indians. He told me of one single-handed adventure he had along this line.

One day a bunch of Comanches rode up to his ranch to relieve him of the care of some of his well-known horses. Leaping bareback on to a little Spanish mule, which was the only animal he had under control at the time, he grabbed off his hat and charged yelling down on those Indians.

"Avancé, compañeros!"

Thinking that he was supported by a band of rangers, the redskins retreated on the dead run, leaving the captain to a more leisurely retirement, his reputation intact, and the "rangers" filed away in his memory for future reference.

Wallace was still pretty active when I first met him in San Antonio, where he spent a good deal of time playing Spanish monte. He would no more qualify for teaching Sabbath school than any of the other old-timers I met, but to me they were all exceedingly interesting. And they got done many things that needed doing.

IV : SHORTHORN COWBOY

One day I was wandering about San Antonio, keeping my ears open for news of a job I might try to get, when I happened to meet the foreman of the Ben Slaughter ranch, who was in the city to employ "brush poppers," or cow hunters. Although to John Longworth I was only a tenderfoot, he hired me.

We did not get away from San Antonio for several days. The principal reason for this was Longworth's desire to enjoy a few of the pleasures the city offered, before returning to the strictly serious atmosphere of the ranch.

In those days the theaters and dance halls were packed every night with hard riders from the cattle ranges, as well as other gentry. In the numerous crowded gambling halls the ceiling was the limit, and everyone seemed to have money he wanted to be rid of. John Longworth spent a good deal of time drinking and playing Spanish monte.

Being a "shorthorn kid" in that country, I could only look on and take in the excitement. Sometimes, while waiting for Longworth to go sufficiently broke to be ready to leave town, I would ride along the San Antonio River a few miles, enjoying the beauty of the country that was so new to me.

Finally my new foreman, or caporal, was ready to leave for the ranch, situated in the brush country to the southwest, and we started out, taking with us some pack ponies loaded with provisions and a few cooking utensils. Longworth had hired several riders, all Mexicans except me. He spoke Spanish fluently, but I understood not a word. As we rode along, I did become familiar with a song he sang repeatedly about "San Antonio Querido." When not singing, our caporal seemed to me a surly man, and I found out soon enough that he was a vicious and dangerous one; but he was a good vaquero, adept at brush running.

About four days from San Antonio we reached Dog Town, the capital of the brush country, on the Frio River. The town obviously got its name from the numberless Mexican dogs that overran it; the population consisted chiefly of Mexican families, each of which owned several dogs. It was the habit of these animals to snap at the heels of every cowboy's pony — apparently for the pleasure of seeing the horses so attacked put on an exhibition of pitching, which they always did.

Cowboys generally rode into town on days when the mail hack was due. This was usually drawn by six half-wild mules, which had to be checked by a helper at every station before they would come to a halt. Any passenger who wished to disembark between stations was strictly on his own; he had to jump with his baggage as best he might, the driver being able to help only to the extent of circling the mules. There was a thrill to be had in riding the mail hack.

The stage line was divided into what corresponds to the divisions on a railroad in these times. At the last station on the division, the driver usually changed to a good coach, which he drove into San Antonio. Out on the road he was not particular, using an ordinary hack and only four animals, unless six were necessary. But when the mail reached the city, it was with the driver atop a coach with all the trimmings, and six wild little mules swinging it around the corners on two wheels. City hacks soon learned to clear out of its way. It seemed to be the particular pride of these early-day drivers to create a sensation. Down the street they would come, whips cracking, animals on a dead run, while people scampered to right and left.

His whip was the stage driver's most prized possession. He clung to it by day, and slept with it at night. Indeed, he had two — one of buckskin, and the other of rawhide. The buckskin whip was finely braided, sometimes of sixteen strands;

but it was useless when wet. For rainy spells a whip of rawhide soaked in tallow was used.

We traveled on past Dog Town, and finally reached the Slaughter ranch. Ben Slaughter had emigrated from Mississippi first to the eastern part of the Lone Star land, and on later to western Texas, where from 1865 he lived in the region afterwards organized into La Salle County. He had three sons whom I never saw at the home ranch — only in camps. Later they became important drovers on the trail from Texas to Kansas.

We made camp a short distance from the ranch house, which was just a jacal, or shack, such as the Mexicans built. It was ten or twelve feet square, made of mesquite poles set in the ground, with other poles and brush for a roof. There was a fireplace on one side. Around the house was a low fence of willows interwoven with brush. The vaqueros and their families lived in small settlements along the streams.

We had started to make camp when a little old man walked down from the ranch house. He wore a belt filled with Henry rifle cartridges, and the handle of a big butcher knife stuck out of one of his boot tops. Thinking he was a Mexican, I used my whole Spanish vocabulary, picked up from Longworth on the way, trying to say "good evening" to him. When I had ceased my efforts to use a couple of simple Spanish words, he looked me over a moment, and said, "Yes, it is a mighty pretty evenin'." Then he turned to Longworth and began to talk in a combination of Spanish and English. This man, I discovered, was Ben Slaughter!

Those Texas pioneers belonged to that class of men who have constituted the real vanguard of our American civilization — a venturesome few who, regardless of danger and privations, moved with their families far out from the settlements to establish their homes and ranches. They loved the life, and required little in the way of raiment, food, and shelter to make them content.

Cooking was done on open fires, either in crude fireplaces or out of doors. Dutch ovens, camp kettles and coffee pots made of sheet iron, and frying pans were all their utensils. They used tin plates and cups, and those ranchmen who had women folk about used iron knives, forks, and spoons. When other eating tools were lacking, the butcher knife which every man carried served all dining purposes. Home or camp fires had to be kept burning, and matches were seldom, if ever, used; fires were made with flint and steel and tinder made of lint or cotton or fuse or punk (dry, rotted wood). Neither did Texas frontiersmen have wheat flour — cornmeal was used and enjoyed by the first white folks of Texas.

Game and livestock were plentiful. A cattleman could quickly increase his stock of cattle and horses by putting his earmark and brand on unbranded animals. If he was not skilled in catching wild stock, he could secure the services of

Mexican vaqueros, who for small wages and some ammunition, tobacco, or a little calico, would do the catching and branding for him.

Handling cattle and horses was native to the vaqueros. From the time when the Spanish landed the first cattle and horses on American shores, the Indians and Mexicans had been trained in the life of the cowboy.

During the early days of the cattle business ranchmen could find market mainly only for hides and tallow; prior to 1850 there was practically no demand for longhorn beef beyond the southwest ranges. Hides became leather goods — shoes, saddles, bridles, belts, and other useful commodities — while tallow was in demand for making soap and candles. The meat of cattle slaughtered for tallow and leather was fed to razor-back hogs, which in turn were transformed into pork and shipped to New Orleans and other cities.

Pioneers settling on Texas frontiers captured enough of the vast numbers of longhorns and horses which roamed wild through the brush country to serve their need for beef and for saddle animals — the inbred Spanish horses had become the mustangs of the West. The settlers had little need for money, but when they did, they might occasionally sell a few cowhides, deerskins, or leopard cat pelts. It wasn't until a railroad was built into Kansas following the Civil War, and a market for the longhorns established, that the cattle industry in Texas became a profitable business.

When I went into Texas in the early eighteen-seventies, hundreds of thousands of cattle were being driven from the Lone Star land to the grazing lands farther north. Millions of Americans have eaten this frontier beef, fattened and shipped eastward from ranches that developed on northern ranges; and great quantities of it have been exported to the countries across the sea.

Cattle began to be sold by ranchers in Texas to buyers who collected big herds and trailed them to the northern markets. With the growing demand for longhorns, Texas cattlemen began to take increased interest in their respective brands and earmarks. Some of them, like Ben Slaughter, employed Mexicans to enclose large tracts of land with stout fences, built of poles cut from the thickets through which the fences were constructed. So strong were these fences that cattle seldom broke through except in a mass stampede. Thousands of acres so enclosed became known to the pioneers by special names — the Indian Bend, the Douraty, and the Cotulea were among the big pastures.

It required a force of trained cow hunters to get wild longhorns out of the thickets of brush and cactus of the open plains into the pastures. Training them to be herded day and night was another task that took skill and patience. It was no easy work to be a brush popper. There was hard riding in it for all.

V : RAWHIDE

I had a talk — in English — with Mr. Slaughter later that first evening. He said he would pay me two dollars a month more than the Mexicans he employed, which meant that my wages would be ten dollars a month, board included. All I had to do was to earn my money, an undertaking for which I didn't have long to wait.

Very early the next morning, while the stars still shone, we were astir. If I had little idea about my work, I did know how to eat my breakfast of pork and cornbread. After the meal Longworth and two or three of the Mexicans rode to a pasture a short distance away and brought in a bunch of forty to fifty saddle horses. All hands went to the corral into which the animals had been driven, where the caporal divided the horses among us, pointing out four or five which were to be mine. I looked them over carefully, so as to be sure I would recognize them, for each cowboy used only the horses assigned to him.

Longworth then lassoed one of my ponies and told me to saddle up. I did. When I tightened the cinch, the pony jumped into the air and tried to turn cartwheels. A little lump rose in my throat, but I gathered my courage and finally managed to get into the saddle. The pony had no further objections to make. He proved a good cow horse, but he was certainly a bluffer to a stranger, and I was relieved when he trotted off without trying to sun my moccasins. The others, all expert riders and ropers, had little trouble with their mounts.

When all were ready we went to a pasture, rode around about fifty head of cattle, and drove them to camp; this, Longworth told me, was to be decoy herd. Later I found out what he meant.

Those longhorns would not have been called gentle in any part of the country save western Texas. They had not long been separated from the wild herds, and were just "gentle" enough to be accustomed to the sight of a man on horseback, so that they could be controlled somewhat by riders. It required little to frighten them, and they expressed their fear in terms of rage that knew no bounds; when brought to bay, they were exceedingly dangerous to deal with.

The caporal drew a rifle from the scabbard on his saddle, and looked over the herd carefully for a likely animal for beef. Ben Slaughter, who had ridden out to us, rode past and called, "What's the matter? Can't John find a fat one?"

At that moment I spied a fine heifer at the edge of the herd, and pulling out my Spencer carbine, I leveled it at the animal (not intending to shoot unless Mr. Slaughter ordered me to).

"There's a good one," I said.

"Hold on, young man; hold on!" yelled the boss, starting his horse toward me on the run. "Don't you see that that's a T-Diamond?"

"Yes," I replied. "Whose brand is that?"

"I reckon it's my brand," he answered. "We don't kill that kind in this country. Kill an L O W or a W B C (any brand but his own); they taste better!"

By this time Longworth had selected a beef that suited him, and he fired, but failed to kill it. Another shot or two from his gun only wounded the animal still further, and by this time the herd was milling around threateningly, badly frightened by the firing and the antics of its wounded member. A lariat thrown on the wounded beast by one of the Mexicans snapped like a bit of string under the terrible jerks of the longhorn.

The now infuriated animal charged in the direction of Mr. Slaughter and me. Taken by surprise, and somewhat excited by this unexpected move, I impulsively grabbed my carbine, while Mr. Slaughter spurred his pony out of harm's way. The brute was within six feet of me when I fired a ball which struck it in the center of the forehead, killing it instantly. I was pretty proud of that shot, though it was more good luck than anything

The infuriated animal charged in the direction of Mr. Slaughter and me.

else. Mr. Slaughter turned in his saddle and said, "I reckon you'll do to help fight Comanches!"

The herd was returned to the corral. After the slain beef was dressed, such portions of it as were desired were hung up in the mesquite trees near camp.

One of the things I learned quickly was that because of the abundance of cattle, and also because the weather was too warm to keep meat longer than a day or two, only the choicest parts of an animal were eaten. I have helped to kill many cattle just for their ribs and hides. It was a common thing to kill a beef each day in a cow camp. The meat was generally cooked by weaving one end of a long pointed green stick through it and thrusting the other end in the earth, before a good bed of mesquite or live oak coals.

We put in the rest of the day making hobbles for our saddle horses. Whenever cowboys had any spare time, they spent it working on articles needed in their work.

Making hobbles, or reatas, or other necessary articles of the cowboy's equipment, is one thing; making a word picture of the process is another. First, a green hide was stretched tightly between stakes on the ground, and thoroughly dried. Then, with someone holding the hide straight and taut, a man would cut through the hide at the desired width with a very sharp knife, sometimes using a notched stick for a guide. The strip was cut spirally, working from the outside of the hide inward. Then one end of the strip was attached to a tree, and the cutter would scrape the hide clean of hair, working in the direction in which the hair grew, not against it.

Depending upon the width to which it had been cut, the strip was now ready to be made into hobbles, lassos, quirts, or reins. During any of these processes, the rawhide was at all times kept thoroughly wet.

The strip used in making hobbles was two or three inches wide. One end of the strip was folded over twice, and a slit was made down the center of the three thicknesses of the fold. A marlin-spike was forced through this slit to separate the sides so that the other end of the strip could be pulled through to make a loop, which was put around a stick about the size of a horse's leg. The ends were then twisted around each other and thrown around another piece of stick placed a foot or two from the first, and the hobble was left to dry at this length. We tried to make a set of hobbles last for the duration of a spell in camp or on the trail. Hobbling fifty to a hundred saddle ponies every night was no small task.

For making a lasso, usually of four strands, a hide of even thickness was selected, for like a chain, a lasso is no stronger than its weakest point. One end of each forty-foot strand was made fast to a limb, and the rawhide was plaited, great care being taken to have the same tension on each wet strand. Then with each end securely fastened to a tree, the lasso, or reata, was stretched and allowed partly to dry. It was then rolled out with a boot sole on a flat rock or log. The maker rubbed it full of an oily yellow fat from a cow.

The hondo, or circle at one end which helped to make the lasso, was a separate part, attached to the reata later. It was made by wrapping a narrow strip of selected hide around a stick, leaving an inside diameter in the coil of from one to two inches, depending on the size of the rope and the inclination of the maker. A slit was cut in the folds, the ends of the reata were pulled through it for a foot or so, and a Spanish knot was tied in all four strands and pulled back down so that the knot rested firmly against the inside of the coil. When soaked and dried and shaped into the form desired, this made a strong and serviceable hondo. As the greatest wear came on the hondo, a reata often outwore three or four of them. Sometimes the hondo was made from the very thick hide from the throat of a bull, the throat being the part of nearly all creatures which Nature has seen fit to protect most carefully.

A short rope was preferred in the brush. A trained brush hunter never tied knots in the tail of a rawhide rope; it was left straight, and plaited so that it looked like the rattles of a rattlesnake. In roping wild cattle or horses it was bad enough to receive a blow with a flat rope; but to get one from a knot or to have a knot entangle the rope in the brush might bring serious injury. It was considered the earmark of a tenderfoot to tie such a knot in his reata, or to loop it at both ends.

Quirts were made in the same manner as lassos, but with eight plaited strands, round and tapered. The handle was a little sack of buckskin filled with shot. All sorts of fancy knots were used, at the whim of the maker. Vaqueros carried the quirt on the middle finger when it was not on the horn of the saddle; to carry it on the wrist was dangerous — we would rather lose a quirt than a hand, should the quirt become caught in the brush.

It was all new work to me, but before many months had passed I could work up rawhide into hobbles, reatas, quirts, and reins. Some vaqueros were very expert in tying Spanish knots and plaiting rawhide and leather, an accomplishment probably acquired from Spanish sailors. I too learned to do all sorts of knot-tying, braiding, or plaiting. The Mexicans were all very kind to me, seeming to derive pleasure from trying to teach me. It was not long before I had picked up a little of their language, particularly such words as pertained to the work. They gave me the name "Santiago," which stuck by me until I left the brush country.

I began to realize that I was sure enough on the frontier. Everybody went armed to the teeth at all times; there was danger on all sides, and from many sources. No man removed his coat or brush jacket when he lay down to sleep. Light sleeping soon became my habit.

In San Antonio I had purchased at a pawnshop a bowie knife of great weight, on the blade of which was engraved this inscription:

Never draw me without cause, nor sheathe me without honor

I must have fallen readily into the spirit of the times, for as I rested that night in camp, waiting for the hour when we should start after wild cattle, I lay wondering who or what would be the first victim of that blade. I don't think I was bloodthirsty, but I was bound that should any man, red or white, attempt to secure my scalplock, I would do my best to protect it.

I had come from a region where people had accepted, and as a rule lived up to, the Ten Commandments; a region where, when trouble arose between men, the settlement seldom cost more than a few bruises. On the frontier different conditions prevailed. The wilds of this land of chaparral and cactus were the refuge of many who had committed all sorts of desperate crimes. There was little employment for these rough men other than working with stock, so that naturally they took to the life of the cowboy, when they were not occupied in dodging Texas Rangers or robbing stages and small settlements. The law seldom entered the brush country, and when it did, the outlaw was more likely than not to have the best of it. A majority of the ranchmen preferred aiding a white criminal to helping bring him to justice. This preference sprang from a motive of self-protection, for the enmity of such characters was a most dangerous thing to invite. Almost their every dispute was settled with the gun or the knife, or by assassination. Such criminals, the thieving bands of Mexicans and Indians, the wild beasts of all sorts, the centipedes, tarantulas, and the snakes, combined to make life a matter for alert interest on my part.

One cannot help admiring the courage of the people who made the conquest of our wild frontiers. By their daring and determination the country was gradually subdued, and made productive and law-abiding. Out of it have come many Americans who have helped in the building of the nation.

VI : BRUSH POPPER

The caporal started his crew on a cow hunt early the day following my first experience at getting beef and at making hobbles. We were quite an outfit — Longworth, ten Mexicans and myself, saddle horses, pack mules, and ponies to carry provisions, and the decoy herd we had rounded up the day before. The pack animals carried greenberry coffee, corn meal, saleratus, salt and pepper berry — no sugar — two Dutch ovens, a frying pan, a camp kettle or two, and a coffee pot. Each man had a pint-size tin cup, and an iron knife and fork.

A pack train generally carried a plentiful supply of black navy plug tobacco, and some prepared corn husks for cigarette papers. Smoking material had to be purchased either at the Slaughter ranch or from Mexican traders traveling over the trail from Laredo to San Antonio. Each man started fires or "made a smoke" with a flint and steel and a piece of punk or prepared cotton tape.

We made our camp near an old corral about five miles from home; this was the base from which we were to do our hunting. What time we had left that day we spent repairing the corral and the wings, to be ready for any wild cattle that we might catch.

In the brush country all corrals were built more or less alike. A trench about three feet deep was dug; strong posts about ten feet long were placed on end in it, close together, and the ground tamped firmly about them. About five feet above ground the posts were lashed together with long strips of green cowhide, which in drying would bind like a vise. Gateposts and bar poles were very strong; when wild cattle were in the corral the bar poles were lashed to the gateposts with ropes.

Strongly built wings were run out sometimes two hundred or more yards from the gate to aid the riders in penning stock.

Next morning about sunrise we rode away with the decoy herd, with Longworth piloting the way through the thick growth of chaparral and mesquite. About a mile away from camp he led the herd into a dense clump of brush, motioning to us to stop driving it.

He left two men with the cattle, and signaled the rest of us to follow him. I fell in line behind the other riders; this, I thought, would be the best position from which to watch what was about to take place.

Suddenly, after we had ridden single file for probably two miles, I heard a crash, and in less than two seconds, every rider ahead of me was riding as if the devil were after him.

My horse knew his work, and plunged after the others. Instinctively I had held him up for a moment; but then the thought struck me that if I didn't keep those men in sight I might never see camp again, for I had not kept track of the direction in which we had been riding, and one acre of brush, timber, and cactus looked like all the rest to me. Therefore, giving my horse the reins, I trailed the ones ahead, guided by the crashing of dead brush and limbs.

I think I rode all over that pony — first on one side, then on the other, and at times, when he would dive under some big live oak limb, I would be almost under his neck. He was a cow-catcher by training. Certainly he made me "pull leather," and I clung to his mane as well, in order to keep in close touch with him. I dodged branches large enough to knock me from my horse, and used an arm to ward from my face smaller limbs and brush. We crossed several prickly pear patches where the clumps grew from two to ten feet high and about as close together as they could stand. My pony would jump over, knock down, or run through them.

I had almost from the beginning of this mad chase an extremely strong desire that it might end, and at last it did. I was in at the finish.

All at once I came in sight of one of the Mexicans. His horse was standing very still. Putting up his hand for me to stop (which I was quite glad to do), he pointed to the brush ahead, where I caught a glimpse of some cattle.

Then there began the sound of voices singing a peculiar melody, a melody without words — the "Texas Lullaby," which the herders used to soothe wild cows. The singers seemed to be scattered in a circle about the cattle.

The longhorns began to come toward me. I recognized a few of them as belonging to the herd we had brought from camp; and in a few seconds more, I saw that we had some wild ones, too.

They whirled back when they saw me, only to find a rider at their rear; they found a rider wherever they turned. The decoy cattle were fairly quiet, milling around through the thicket, and soon mingling thoroughly with the wild ones.

Now every man began to ride very carefully, very slowly, round and round the herd, all singing the strange melody. For all I know, I may have tackled that singing trick right then and there. I was about as excited as those captured longhorns.

After we had ridden around the cattle for an hour or more, I saw Longworth ride out of sight of the herd, dismount, and tighten his cinch. When he returned to the herd, others followed his example. Having had a badly needed breathing spell, our horses were in shape for another run.

The caporal rode away into the chaparral, singing. The Mexicans began driving the cattle after him, pointing them in the direction of his voice when the brush was too thick for him to be seen. I brought up the rear. We kept quite a little distance from the cattle, and each man tried to avoid sudden moves or sounds that might start a stampede.

At last Longworth led us back to camp, and the wild cattle followed the decoys through the wings and into the corral. The heavy bar poles were lashed. We had caught some wild cattle.

I had had a most thrilling experience; now I began to count the cost. My clothing was pretty well torn off, and likewise a goodly portion of my skin; about nine varieties of thorn were imbedded in my anatomy. I was more than ready for camp. So were all hands, men and horses. Such work was a bit hard on both; but horseflesh was cheap, and certainly no man who didn't enjoy the work would allow himself to be hired to do it.

The caporal who led a string of riders out to gather in wild longhorns had not only to keep a sharp lookout for cattle in the brush; he also had to listen sharply for sounds of breaking brush or running hoofs; and he kept an eye on the ground for fresh tracks. To get around a bunch of wild longhorns, and then to circle them into the thicket containing the decoy herd, meant taking chances. It was a case of trusting in Providence — and then in addition, riding as fast as horseflesh could carry one, regardless of all obstacles. From the second the wild cattle saw, heard, or smelled a human being, it was just "Go!"

The horses were trained to such work, and could detect the presence of cattle more quickly than could even expert brush hunters; and they did their best to help in the capture of longhorns. All a rider had to do was to stick to his horse, and avoid limbs of trees that might strip him and his saddle from his eager mount.

This in itself was no small accomplishment. Yuccas large and strong enough to impale a man on their dagger-like points were a source of danger for which we had to keep a sharp lookout. Occasionally a concealed hole would give both horse and rider a bad fall. Now and then a rider would be thrown into a clump of prickly pear cactus; when this happened, he was forced back to camp, to wait for someone to help him get the thorns out. We used the point or edge of a butcher knife, held against the thumb, for this purpose. The work of the brush popper was painful, as well as exciting, rough, and dangerous.

When the horses became jaded, they were exchanged for fresh ones at the ranch pastures. The cow ponies certainly had their share of hard work and injuries, but they seemed to enter into the spirit of the chase with enthusiasm.

Not all cow hunts terminated as successfully as my first one. Many times during my experience the decoy method failed, and sometimes we not only did not make our catch, but we lost our decoys. Some rider, not being able to tell the exact spot where the decoy herd was, and becoming confused by the many turns the wild cattle made him take, would drive the fleeing longhorns right into the decoys, causing a stampede. Then it was "devil take the hindmost."

What the rider usually did then was to single out an animal and try to catch it with his rope. Or, failing because of thick timber or brush to get his rope on it, he might tail down, or *coliar,* the animal. Tailing down a longhorn was accomplished by riding close to its hindquarters and grabbing its tail, then dashing ahead at an angle, throwing the entire weight on the near stirrup at the second when most of the weight of the longhorn was on its front feet. This would throw the longhorn with such force that usually before it could recover from the bad fall, the driver would have it hog-tied — its feet tied together — with a short rope which he carried looped under his belt for this purpose. This had to be done quickly, or trouble would come to the cow waddie.

Gentler methods could not very well have been used. It was a fight for life and liberty on the part of the wild cattle, and they were too large and strong for a man to control by his own strength. Flight would not be uppermost in the animal's mind at such a time. Longhorns would run from ten to twenty miles from a man, but when brought to bay, roped or tailed down, their rage was such that a man had to be alert to protect life and limb. It was horns against pistol sometimes, when a strong animal regained its feet before it could be hog-tied after being tailed down.

Gathering wild cattle by lassoing and tailing them down was a slow method. Longhorns captured in this way could be released only in a decoy herd which had to be driven to them, or if they were tied to the necks of gentle oxen taken to them. Work oxen were trained for this purpose. We had a pair called Speck and Brandy. When captured animals were released from the tie rope and found their feet, old Speck and Brandy would get their share of the excitement, for captured longhorns never submitted gracefully to being led; they tore up more or less brush and ground before the corral was reached, and they could be turned loose with other cattle.

Although if they had been left tied long enough the longhorns' legs would become too numb to allow them to run fast, yet at times when regaining their feet they would charge the nearest live object, and keep right on through a bunch of cattle or line of riders. Then it became necessary to rope and throw them all over again. In such cases a decoy would be roped and thrown too, and the two dragged together and tied to each other with stout ropes and knots that would not slip; this was called "necking" animals.

When a sufficient number of wild cattle had been captured, they would be earmarked and branded and turned into the home pastures. The branding process set the longhorns on the warpath again. With hide tingling from the hot iron, and ears bleeding from a keen knife that had reshaped them, it was a maddened beast that regained its feet, and it would be very likely to charge those who had wrought the injuries. Though its horns were not well adapted for the goring process, nevertheless they could knock a cowboy off his balance and injure him seriously. Horses, too, were sometimes killed or badly gored by an infuriated beast. A horse and rider trapped in a corner of the corral were in grave danger. Men working on foot would make for the nearest corral fence and scale it, when such a feat was possible.

I was at first about as useless and helpless an individual as ever graced a cow camp, so far as helping to control these wild brutes was concerned. I kept my eyes open, though; I was there to stay, if I could only get the hang of the work. After a few weeks I could do a little with a rope, and do my part in controlling the stock. It required the use of brain and eye every moment, and skill in riding. My first months at the Slaughter ranch brought many new and rare experiences. I never saw another white boy my age in the cow camps, taking part as a brush popper.

VII : WILD CATTLE RANGE

We caught wild cattle in other ways than by the decoy system. That method was good in a locality only so long as the longhorns remained in large bunches. However, in nearly every run we made, some cattle got away from us, and these soon learned that the best way to escape was to scatter, and each make its own lone race for liberty. With those that had learned this trick it was necessary to follow another plan.

Under the leadership of our caporal we would ride out very early in the morning, keeping a sharp lookout for sign of a bunch of wild longhorns. Once we found sign, we followed until we came in sight of the bunch, or by chance happened on another herd. Our lassos, or ropes, as they were commonly called by cowboys, were then brought into play. Each rider selected an animal regardless of its age, sex, or color, and attempted to lasso it.

The task undertaken by a rider when he set sail

after one of those cow critters was far from being an easy one. Longhorns had a long running gear, and their bodies were not very wide. Their legs could carry them at a rate of speed which made even a fast horse exert himself to the utmost to overtake one of them. The use of the lasso in catching cattle in thick brush, timber, and prickly pear, required great dexterity and skill. Some vaqueros acquired remarkable expertness.

Ten feet or more of the thirty-foot lasso were taken up by the loop thrown — and in very thick brush only a very small loop could be thrown; a larger one would catch on some object and prevent a good throw, or it might wind around some strong shrub or limb, and bring the horse to a sudden stop, sometimes even breaking the cinch. A rider failing to get the loop of his lasso on the head or legs of the longhorn he was chasing might spur alongside the animal and tail it down, rather than take time to make his lasso ready again.

When, without decoys, we jumped a bunch of wild cattle in some thicket it was every man for himself: catch 'em and tie 'em. Naturally we all became separated in the process, and this was fine training for the "bump of location," for after a catch or a failure, one had to find his own way back to camp, and in case of success had to lead the decoy herd or work oxen back to the captured longhorn. For a person born without a "coyote sense" to lead him back to the meal sack when hungry, that country was a mighty poor place to live.

Another method used to catch wild cattle which had become so smart, or "up to trap," was to hunt them on full moonlight nights. We would remain in camp all day and about sundown ride two miles or so to the edge of some one of the bits of prairie all about us. Keeping ourselves and our horses hidden in the thick brush, we would wait for moonrise.

It wouldn't be long before we would hear a cow low, a calf bawl, or a bull bellow. We might hear also the breaking of brush, as the longhorns filed rapidly into the open. Our horses, which could both see and hear the cattle farther than their riders could, seemed to know that they were getting close, and would fairly tremble with excitement, anticipating the chase to come.

All riders, with girths tightened and ropes ready for a quick throw, would slip into their saddles. The moment the caporal thought the cattle were far enough out on the prairie for us to catch them before they could get back into the dense chaparral, he would give the signal, and like an arrow from a bow, each vaquero would be off after every longhorn on the prairie.

It was a breakneck game, but good sport for those who liked it. Sometimes a man would make a catch just as an animal dashed for the timber. With the noose end of the rope around a big animal's horns, neck, or body, and the other end tied fast to the rider's saddle-horn, and the animal rushing around one side of a tree while the cowboy and his horse took the other side, something had to happen. Either the rope snapped or there was a collision about half the rope's length from the tree. Sometimes a horse would be gored to death in these mix-ups, and a rider had to scramble for dear life.

In these single efforts to capture longhorns the men would become separated. It was our custom to keep up an incessant imitation of a lowing cow, so that unless we were too greatly scattered, we could keep in touch with one another. By this means one of us was occasionally able to aid one of the others, if he had time to spare after tying an animal or losing one.

I well remember one little moonlight cow-chasing expedition. I had tied down the animal I was after, and was sitting on my horse listening for the sound of someone to whom I could be of service. I had not long to wait. First it was only a faint lowing I heard, but it grew louder each moment, indicating that the rider was headed in my direction, probably on an old cow trail which passed near the point where I was stationed.

Clearing my rope for action, I rode behind a bunch of Spanish bayonet plants close by the trail. By this time I knew that something charged ahead of the rider, not more than two hundred yards away. A few seconds later a slick black bull dashed by. I was ready for him and threw my loop over his head just as he passed.

There must have been an extra spring in that

bull's body which he used at that moment, for when he came to the end of my rope, my saddle girth parted with a loud snap, and I went sailing through space, with my feet still in the stirrups. My head bumped the ground.

I never heard from that bull or that saddle again. If the animal kept on at the speed he had attained when my lasso encircled his neck, then by the time I sat up he was somewhere east of Suez. The horse ridden by the bull's pursuer was badly winded, and as the longhorn was gaining ground, there was nothing the Mexican could do to help me recover my saddle and rope. I shouldered my rifle, which luckily had been flung from its scabbard about when I was parting company with the saddle, and returned to camp with the vaquero, with a fine large lump on my head as a souvenir of the occasion. I was soon outfitted with another saddle and rope from the home ranch, and ready for more sport with the playful longhorns.

In writing of these experiences, I realize that it is difficult to make even cattlemen of the present day understand what the expression "wild cattle" meant in those days. Buffalo or deer could have been no wilder. The longhorns would not graze on open ground in the daytime, but would seek the dense thickets or lie with their heads on the ground like deer, listening and sniffing, on the lookout for danger, and always ready for a mad rush through the jungles to safety.

It will be difficult also to make the majority of those who will read this account picture just what was meant by "brush" in that region. In New Mexico and southern Colorado the stubble sage was bad enough to run a horse through; in the cedar brakes of the Llano hills the brush was also bad. Cowboys who learned to catch wild cattle along the Llano River would turn a horse loose over high banks after a cow, in a way that no boy used to brush would dare to do. But put one of the Llano boys after a longhorn in the brush country between the Nueces and the Rio Grande, and he would have the devil's own time catching one, if he ever did.

No tree growth apparently responds more readily to climate than mesquite. In southwest Texas, where it seemed to reach its maximum growth, it developed into great trees. The thorns on the mesquite vary in number and size. In the Brasada, heart of the mesquite country, where growth ranged from little bushes to big trees, the countless thorns were very long and sharp. And mesquite is just one of many thorned growths that were to be encountered in the Brasada. There were thick clumps of the coma, with dagger-like thorns, which in season bore blue berries liked by Mexican doves; Mexicans said that the coo of the doves meant that they wanted to come and eat berries. There were thickets of cejas, of Brasil, and clepino. One bush covered with thorns was believed by Mexicans to have been used in Christ's crown of thorns. Among the dozens of other growths a common one was catsclaw; when it took hold, it never let go.

Numerous other plants added interest and difficulty to brush hunting. The juajilla, spreading over the hills, had small scattered thorns which, however, did not prevent its leaves from being eaten by horses and cattle. Its flowers gave a particularly fine flavor to honey. Wild currant, called agarita, was armed also with spines. It was the first to bud in spring. The armogosa was famous for its use in medicinal tea. The black chaparral grew thick and high and unbroken over thousands of acres. Prickly pear often grew higher than a man on horseback. Rattail cactus and cholla had the most thorns per square inch, and were good mainly to annoy vaqueros. In the winter they were covered by red berries eaten by the Mexican quail. From the Spanish bayonet plant Mexicans obtained a poison which they used as an antidote for rattlesnake bite. All these plants were adapted to the country, and locked thorns, as it were, to prevent intrusion.

Before the cattle became numerous and mesquite grass was dense, Indian fires sometimes swept the ranges to keep the brush in check. But after ranchers established homes there, the brush began to gain possession for hundreds of miles. The more fertile the soil, the more rapidly it spread; the drier the season, the heavier the mesquite bean crop would be. Drought would kill live oaks, but no drought ever eliminated a chaparral jungle. There was enough soil in the crotch of a tree, it was said, for a prickly pear to grow in, if it could contrive somehow to reach it.

To work in this jungle of thorns we had to wear stout clothing. Tapaderos (toe-protectors) for our stirrups, heavy leather boots and leggings, brush jackets, gauntlet gloves, and strong hats, were standard equipment. These were mostly of Mexican manufacture and of good material, which was essential in articles subject to such rough treatment.

Little ornamentation was used on hats. A heavy roll about two inches wide and three-quarters of an inch thick, made of some such springy material as horsehair, was used as a hatband. Crowns were not high, and brims were seldom more than five inches in width. Brim and roll gave some protection to the rider's head. A strong buckskin thong used as a chin-strap served to keep hats from being torn from heads in the thick brush. Chaparejos, or chaps, as they are now called, and high-heeled boots, the most distinctive articles of early American cowboy dress, are still in common use on the cattle ranches.

Clothing, aside from leggings, boots, and hats, was not weighty or at all extensive. We dispensed with underclothing and socks, and achieved the slim effect with a pair of trousers and a cotton shirt. To these we added during our work a brush jacket of leather or strong Mexican cloth, ammunition or cartridge belts, pistols, and bowie knives.

Economy was not the only factor which caused us to go without some of the articles of clothing considered essential today in a cowboy's outfit. During frontier times all soldiers, freighters and cow hunters had to contend with vermin. Mexicans had learned to combat them quite successfully. Their method was to divest themselves of all their clothing and place it on an ant heap, where the busy ants would soon free the clothes of the pests. The Mexicans would then rub lavishly over their bodies soap suds from the root of the yucca plant, and leave it there to dry, in order to destroy any straggling lice or eggs. When utensils were available in which to boil clothing infested with vermin, that method was also employed.

Cowboy hats, boots, and chaps have been improved as to size, style, and beauty since the days when we first wore such things. Wealthy Mexican ranchmen have long worn most expensive and showy hats and clothing. Their ornate and costly saddles, bridles, bits, and spurs, as well as hats and clothing, often have gold and silver trimmings. They took great pride in being accomplished equestrians and skilled users of the lasso. Traces of the influence of such pride and precedent may yet be seen at roundups on the range or at Wild West shows.

VIII : BRONCHO BUSTING

Horses we rode hunting the wild longhorns were almost all descended from the barbs introduced into Spain by the Moors. Cortez brought twenty-five of them as mounts for his conquistadores when he landed in Mexico in 1519. No native horses then existed in North America, so far as is known; the once abundant prehistoric horse had long been extinct. About two years later came some longhorns, and other shipments of cattle and horses followed from Spain. During the after years these animals multiplied and spread over the great stretch of North American territory conquered by the Spaniards.

The little inbred Spanish horses were well adapted for our work. They were not only speedy; they were tough, and able to stand the strain of the sudden stops and turns necessary in working with fractious longhorns. Saddle horses were cheap, although a higher value was set on some which, because of superior training, were particularly useful at all sorts of cowboy work, classifying a herd, roping or tailing down a wild animal.

Ben Slaughter bought hundreds of untrained horses at low prices. Vaqueros at his ranch trained them for the brush-running business. Saddle horses purchased by ranchmen were supposed to be broken to the picket rope and the saddle, to the extent that they could be ridden by one who called himself a rider. The rancher attempted to collect a remuda, or bunch of horses that had been ridden at least a few times. There was little demand for stock horses, such as mares and colts. Our horses were of all colors, and small-sized; a few were perfectly shaped.

Probably three times as many horses were required in the brush as in open country. In brush running our mounts were always being crippled. As long as a horse kept warm he could run, even with a good many thorns in him; but when he cooled off he was stiff and lame. After we had run all day in the brush, many of our horses were sometimes unable to walk to camp. But no matter how tired or run down, at night a horse simply had the saddle jerked off, and was hobbled and turned out to graze.

Mexican vaqueros were not especially humane in handling animals, any more than were the gauchos of South America or the Indians of the plains. The Mexican method of horse training was usually rather rough. A vaquero would ride into a corral with one end of his lasso tied to the horn of his saddle, rope a wild cow, jump off, and leave the horse and the maddened cow to fight it out. The horse might at first get entangled in the lasso, and be injured; but if he had ordinary intelligence, he would locate the cause of his trouble after a few such experiences, and learn to protect himself. Some of the older vaqueros would remain in the saddle and allow the horse to get tangled and jerked down a time or two. Others would tie one end of the rope to a cinch ring instead of the horn, and train the horse to "sit down" with his head toward the lassoed animal. Sitting down was simply squatting, braced sidewise on the hocks against the strain.

My gentle upbringing probably was responsible for the more kindly feeling I had for my horses, compared with the Mexicans' attitude toward theirs. It was not our custom to name our horses, yet to me they were companions. They were of varying intelligence. Occasionally one would sulk when a sudden strain came on him through the jerkings of a wild cow; but most of them seemed to enjoy and take an interest in their work. Much of the horse's skill was dependent on his training and on the rider's skill in handling him in the difficult work.

From the time of my arrival at the Slaughter ranch I rode only the string of ponies assigned to me by our caporal. We did the best we could for our horses. We tried to keep saddle-galls from developing on them. It was a warm country, and such galls might if neglected become "setfasts," or incurable sores, and ruin a horse. It was the caporal's duty to see that a horse with galls that might develop into setfasts was not ridden by a cowboy.

The Mexican "applehorn" saddles we had to use were responsible for many discomforts to our horses. They were far different from the saddles in common use today; their frames, made from the wild apple trees of the islands of Matagorda Bay, were covered with wet rawhide which shrank and tightened when dry, and they were very strong, but hard on the horses. Some of them, being very narrow at the fork, would bruise the withers when wild cattle were being roped, and cause fistulas to start on the horses. In the cowcamps a fistula was considered incurable.

No stock of medicines was available to help keep the horses fit. We had few remedies to cure any kind of saddle sores or other wounds on our hardworking mounts. Where hair was worn off, a little salt pork might be rubbed to start it growing. Poultices of prickly pear and kerosene were sometimes applied to draw out thorns; but no poultice would draw out a viznaga cactus or mesquite thorn.

I felt more companionship for some of my horses than I did for the men I worked with, for though I admired their horsemanship and their skill in capturing cattle, I thought of them as belonging to a different world. Doubtless they felt the same toward me, although occasionally one would show some affection for me, in the form of willingness to do me a kindness.

Felipe, an old employee of the Slaughters, showed me numerous acts of friendship. One day I rode a "fresh horse" — one that had rested a few months, taken on flesh, and very likely acquired a "bad heart," or mean spirit, in the meantime. When I threw my saddle on him, he jumped into the air, fell over backward, and refused to rise. Finally I got him up and climbed into the saddle, but I didn't remain there long. He was an expert bucker, and threw me three times in as many minutes. The last time I was pretty badly hurt, but was starting to get on him again when Felipe came up and took the broncho from me. Though I couldn't understand his words, I knew that he wanted to ride him for me.

"Please tell him I will try again," I said to Longworth, who was near by, seemingly enjoying the sport. He spoke to Felipe in Spanish and walked away, laughing. This determined me that I would master that broncho or die in the attempt.

The next minute the air seemed full of horse, saddle, and boy; how I stuck to the beast, I never knew. When he had quit pitching and I was still on his hurricane deck, I thought he had decided to accept me, but suddenly he stampeded in the direction of some heavy mesquite timber near by. I couldn't check him. Limbs of trees began to strike my face, and I was nearly knocked out of the saddle several times by heavy branches.

I had just made up my mind that the brute would kill me when Felipe came by like a cyclone, grabbed the hackamore rope, took a turn on the horn of his saddle, and brought his horse and mine to a sudden stop.

Blood was running from my nose and mouth. Felipe jumped from his horse, and motioned for me to climb down. Quietly he changed our saddles. Then he led me to a little pool and washed the blood from my face. We went back to camp riding each other's horses. The little horse that had objected so violently to me had similar ideas about Felipe, but was promptly given to understand that a master was on his back, and gave up. In camp I saddled him again, and he gave me no more serious trouble, although he never became what might be considered polite.

One morning I was just climbing back into the saddle after being thrown from a pitching horse, when Jack Woods, who worked for another outfit, rode into camp. He was a rough sort of man who considered it sport to abuse a horse.

"Let me ride that broomtail," he offered.

I climbed out of the saddle. Woods grasped the rope, sidled up to the horse, and jumped into the saddle, the stirrups of which reached only to his knees. Hitting the horse over the head with his hat, he told him to "go to it."

The horse did. He promptly ducked his head

between his hind feet, and did a thorough job of knocking down or running over any and all brush and cactus in the vicinity, while Woods spurred him from ears to tail. When the show was over, the horse stood with his nose to the ground, unable to do any more pitching. (Horses "pitched" in that country; in the North they "bucked.") I realized that Woods had taken the horse, not from any friendship toward me, but because he would rather ride a pitching horse than take part in any other sport.

Our entire bunch of saddle horses, when not being used or driven to fresh camps, was kept hobbled day and night. For some reason horses accustomed to Mexicans and Americans were afraid of Indians. The scent of redskins would cause them to snort and bunch up; sometimes they even hobbled into camp for safety. Indians did occasionally get some of our horses, but to do it they had to employ a good deal of skill. Whenever their thefts became excessive, word would be sent out to other ranches, and a small posse of Americans would attempt to recover the horses and punish the Indians. Mexicans as a rule took little part in hunting Comanche or Apache horse thieves, perhaps because the Indians usually retaliated by raiding little Mexican settlements left defenseless except for old men, while the younger ones worked for the cattlemen. State troopers or rangers took part in the pursuit of Indian horse thieves.

I was certainly out of my element in that wild country, but I did my best to learn the work required of a cow waddie. After a while my Mexican companions aided me to look the part by making a pair of rawhide chaps for me. One of the smaller vaqueros also gave me one of his brush jackets, made of Mexican cloth, so strong that it wore like iron. This gave me at least the outward appearance of a genuine cowhand, probably somewhat earlier than I measured up to the definition in performance, but I was pleased.

IX : MEXICAN VAQUEROS

Vaqueros I met were all descendants of Indian tribes found on the continent by early Spanish explorers — Apaches, southern Comanches, or the Tejas Indians from whom Texas gets its name. They spoke a mixture of native Indian tongues and Spanish.

From the days of the Aztecos, or Aztecs, the majority had felt none too friendly toward white men, but I, being a boy and therefore not classified as a warrior or a Tejano (a native Texan, whom they considered an enemy), was never mistreated by any vaquero. I took great interest in learning from them what I could of their language, sign talk, ways of hunting, caring for hides, cooking, and other customs. Much that I learned from my early association with these people helped me in my life among them, and in my later dealings with the various Indian tribes I was to encounter through the years.

The forefathers of the vaqueros had used bows

and arrows, as well as snares, in capturing game, and the vaqueros of my time had not progressed far in the implements of their trade. Some could throw knives expertly to get game, and they were skilled fighters with that weapon.

As Mexicans far outnumbered other workers in the cow camps, Spanish was the language commonly spoken. Those old-time vaqueros used little profanity, and what they did employ they learned mainly from white men. When they missed with the lasso they might say, *"Baladi Dios!"* but not in a profane sense; the literal translation would be, "God failed me!" When excited in a chase they would yell, *"Yo soy su rey, mi caballo sin segundo, en todos partes del mundo."* ("I am your king, my horse is without a second, in all parts of the world.") My own yell had no words that I can recall, but when I accompanied some of the boys into town after supplies I could screech in a way that won me a reputation.

The vaqueros would pass some of the time around the campfire singing and telling stories. One old Spanish legend they told me ran somewhat like this:

"Long ago, a hunchbacked boy lived in a small village where other boys of his age resided. These companions made the unfortunate boy very unhappy with unkind remarks about his deformed back. One day, to escape their jibes, he determined to run away from the village and seek a better home in some distant land.

"With a little food secured from his parents' larder, he climbed from his bedroom window near the midnight hour, and walked away in the darkness. It did not matter what direction he took, for his only thought was to escape from his tormentors. On through all the next long day he walked, until at nightfall he finally stopped and lay down to rest.

"Later he was awakened by a multitude of singers chanting over and over the words, *'Lunes, y Martes, y Miercoles, tres; Lunes, y Martes, y Miercoles, tres.'* ('Monday, and Tuesday, and Wednesday, three.')

"The boy rose from the ground and started toward the singers. Reaching the top of a hill he peered over and saw Hell, with a great number of devils dancing in the flames, and repeating the words of the song in an ascending scale.

"Thinking to assist the singers by adding to the words they sang, the hunchbacked boy stood up on the hill in plain view, and as they finished with *"'Miercoles, tres,'* he sang out in the wonderful voice he possessed, *'Jueves, y Viernes, y Sabado, seis!'* ('Thursday and Friday and Saturday, six!')

"*'Seis'* rhymed well with *'tres,'* pleasing the singers greatly; so the dancing devils gladly added the words to their song, and the melody descended with a flourish. Quickly capturing the boy, they sang the new song with him, over and over. Then listening to his story, they transformed his back by magic into a normal condition, presented him with a fine new suit and a purse filled with gold coins, and told him how he could return quickly to his village.

"The happy boy, following their directions, was soon back home. His parents and former associates were astonished at his improved appearance, and at the well-filled purse he brought back from his adventure.

"Another hunchbacked boy of the same village, hearing of his good fortune, asked the previously deformed boy how he could get similar results. Given the secret, this boy soon left the village and walked to the hill from which, sure enough, he caught a glimpse of Hell, and heard the devils singing their improved song. Waiting until they finished the last word, he stood up and shouted, *'Domingo, siete!'* meaning 'Sunday, seven.'

"This not only did not rhyme with the other lines, but it produced a discordant sound. Again the devils rushed out, but when they captured the hopeful boy, this time it was displeasure that they felt, and they punished him by playing a cruel trick on him with their magic. Not only did they leave his deformity on his back; they added the hump taken from the other boy, and they sent him off in the opposite direction from his former home."

We talked also of our work, or of Indian fighting. There was little else to divert the mind. No reading matter or mail reached us, and we had no communication with the rest of the world.

We hardly knew what year it was, and the month or day meant nothing. It was a little world of our own in which we lived.

There were no regular paydays. When we needed clothing, ammunition, or tobacco, they were purchased and sent to us by our employers. Years might go by before a cowhand would have a wage settlement with his employer. I never heard of anyone being cheated in his wages; there existed implicit trust on the part of the vaqueros. So far as I know, they kept no account of what was due them, except in their heads. Some, however, had excellent memories, and it was dangerous to try to cheat them. They were honest and true as steel to their employers. It was the custom on the frontier to take a man's word, without requiring signatures to back it.

Especially during the rainy season, we needed shelter badly, but we had little protection. We could live out in the open without much discomfort during the summer months, when it was very dry, but when the marrow-piercing northers swept the land with their chilling rain and wind, we cowhands surely had an unhappy time. I never saw a cow hunters' camp where any provision was made for protecting the men from the bite of wind and rain.

We were expected to stand any sort of weather a cow critter could stand. The cows, I think, had the better of the deal, for their hides were thick and tough, and well covered with a thatch of hair, while the poor vaquero had to protect himself from the elements with only his scant clothing and one blanket, usually of poor quality and worn threadbare. Bed tarpaulins had not been introduced, and tents were not to be had.

The timber or brush we sought when hard rains came gave poor shelter. There was no after-supper singing or story-telling then. If the rain fell so fast that the campfire failed us, we went without food and coffee, and there was little joy in our hearts. Our ammunition and little stock of cornmeal, saleratus, and pepper berries were protected by an old wagon sheet or a grease-filled cowhide or two. We slept with our clothes on, although we sometimes removed our boots and placed them under our heads, where they could be reached quickly.

Some few cowhands owned good, hard-woven blankets with a slit in the middle large enough for a man's head to slip through. Such a blanket, or poncho, together with a well-made Mexican sombrero, gave considerable protection from rain and wind; the prosperous few who could afford these wore them proudly in city and country. But most of us poor brush poppers had to take the storms as they came. If there were trees near camp, each man selected one and leaned or sat with his back against it, his blanket wrapped about him, while the rain came down, down, down.

Rain gave us only one advantage — elimination

of danger from Indians. It was not during the stormy moons that we had need to sleep with our boots on, watchful that our saddle ponies did not change hands in the night. Comanches and Apaches appeared to care more for the white man's horse than for his religion; but they cared less for the driving rain. It was usually on full moonlight nights, when the sky was not cloudy, that they roamed the country trying to steal horses, or to waylay and kill men for ammunition or guns.

There were other things to disturb the slumbers of the cowboy, such as the rush of a band of stampeded, hobbled horses into camp; or occasionally the prickling sensation of a centipede working its way along the body of a sleeping man. One would do several kinds of fancy steps in ridding oneself of this close-clinging pest. Wild beasts were all about us, but they gave us little trouble unless molested. However, we were occasionally disturbed by wolves.

One night we were all lying around the camp trying to get some sleep when a wolf stole in among us. Longworth moved in his sleep, swinging his arm. Its attention attracted, the wolf leaped for him and seized his arm in its powerful teeth. Yelling, Longworth grabbed and held the beast with his free hand, until he could pull a knife from its scabbard and stab the wolf to death.

The thought of hydrophobia worried us, and the Mexicans took some big leaves of the prickly pear cactus growing nearby, burned off the spines,

split the leaves, and bound them on the l
This procedure may have prevented serious results, or it may have been that the wolf's teeth had been freed of virus in passing through the brush jacket and other clothing the caporal wore. At any rate, no bad results other than a sore arm followed the attack.

I don't know just what medicinal value the vaqueros' remedies had. To me there was some sense in the procedure they followed with a wound such as was made by a bullet, which was to insert a grain of black pepper berry both where the bullet entered and where it left the body. Probably the action of the hot pepper kept the wound from healing on the outside until the infection within had cleared.

A cowboy was likely to receive injuries at any time in the normal course of his daily work. His lasso, if it became damp from rain and was not as pliable as usual, would keep forming little loops in which the cowboy could easily lose a finger or a hand if he was not careful. A time or two I had my own hand caught and the skin stripped off by a refractory lasso.

The lasso was a dangerous fighting weapon. Many Mexicans used their reatas in fighting duels. Such affairs were strictly serious and in deadly earnest. The idea of each fighter was to get the rope around any part of his rival's body — preferably his neck — and then to whirl his horse, jerk the man out of his saddle, and drag him to death.

I saw one such encounter. Two vaqueros who had quarreled while in town attending a fandango were still such enemies when they returned to camp that they agreed to fight it out in a duel on horseback with lassos. I heard little of their conversation, but I saw them get on their horses and ride apart about a hundred yards. Suddenly they whirled their horses and started full speed toward each other, swinging their loops. Several throws were warded off by each, but at last one landed his loop over the other, and succeeded in dragging him out of the saddle, whereupon he started his horse as fast as it could run. The unfortunate Mexican was dragged over and through everything in the way. It took about two minutes, I think, to kill him. When it was over the other vaqueros went out, got his body, and buried him.

John Longworth once ended a misunderstanding with a Mexican cowhand in much the same way, although not with the same sportsmanship. When they got out of the brush the caporal, angered at something that had happened, stole up behind the vaquero and managed to slip the loop of his lasso quickly over the man's head. Whirling his horse, he jerked him from his saddle, probably breaking his neck, and dragged him a little way to make sure he was dead. The rest rode away from the scene, not daring even to care for the body, for all knew Longworth's temper. Human life was held very cheap then by some.

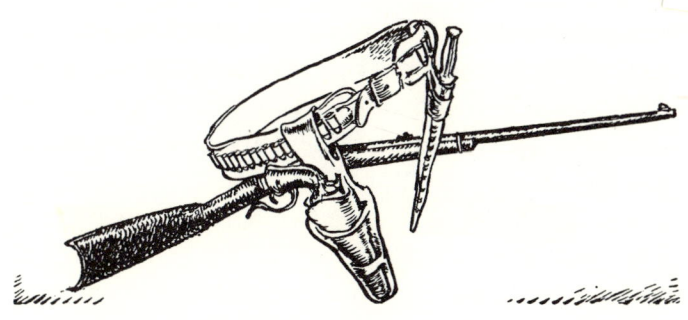

X : GUNS AND GAME

Most of the white men who inhabited southwest Texas when I was there were armed with Colt or Remington muzzle-loading revolvers of the type used by soldiers of the Civil War. Frontiersmen of that time considered these "six-shooters" most reliable for either warfare or shooting scrapes between white men. They were very accurate weapons. As fixed ammunition in the way of metallic cartridges began to appear, these earlier cap-and-ball revolvers gradually were discarded. Some of the non-progressive old frontiersmen, however, did not take kindly at first to this new-fangled invention, declaring that they wanted to know what was being fed into their guns.

I had a muzzle-loading Colt, and by chance I secured also a copper flask made especially for use with the revolver. This flask would contain six charges of powder, and had a shut-off measuring gauge to regulate the amount of powder, as well as a compartment that held six bullets (we made our own bullets). It was small enough to be carried in my trousers pocket, and so became a handy device to help me load my six-shooter more quickly and accurately. It was the only powder flask of the kind I ever saw.

As a saddle gun I used a Spencer carbine at first, but it was not an especially good weapon, and I was happy when an opportunity came to trade it for a better one. A Mexican rode into camp one day with a Henry rifle, almost new, for which he wanted to buy cartridges. We had none, but we did have some ammunition for my rifle, and I succeeded in trading my Spencer and some ammunition for his Henry. Later I got from Mr. Slaughter some cartridges for my new gun. It proved to be a most accurate shooting-piece — as good, I felt, as any in use in Texas at the time.

No one armed with a good rifle ever suffered for want of meat in the brush country. Even with bow and arrows one might bring down some of the plentiful game. An ordinary cowhand or vaquero seldom owned a rifle or a revolver; yet no matter how poor he might be, each was generally armed with a sheath knife, and was expert in getting game with it.

With my Henry rifle I could shoot the head off a rabbit, or get as many wild turkeys as I needed. Great flocks of this king of all game fowl roamed about, feeding during daylight hours, and at night roosting in large trees near the waterways. Sometimes their roosting places extended a quarter of a mile, so large were the flocks. Often I watched them fly up from somewhere in the thickets, into the pecan or live oak trees on the banks of the Nueces or the Frio.

I have shot more than one big wild gobbler from its perch thirty or forty feet above our campfire. By the light of the campfire I would pluck and dress them, and cut them in pieces of a size that would enable me to get the whole bird into our largest camp kettle. With the lid from one of our Dutch ovens for a cover, I would put the kettle on a bed of live mesquite coals several inches deep. By breakfast time the meat would be boiled from the bones, and taking a piece of cold corn bread left from supper, I would dip into the rich broth while eating a turkey feast fit for a king. My iron fork prevented my fingers from being burned, but probably my waist measure suffered considerably from such an indulgence.

There were many other edible game birds. Quail were abundant, and never having been hunted, they were not so wild as they are today. When I wanted quail, I would shoot a couple and broil them on a green stick over a bed of hardwood coals. Other tasteful shore game birds to be found at certain seasons around the lagoons and bayous suffered the same fate from my rifle.

Wild hogs were numerous. The meat of the little javalinas and slab-sided razorbacks was enjoyed as a delicacy, and leather from their stout hides served to make leggings and brush jackets.

A big hog's head cooked Mexican-Indian style I considered a treat. A pit about two and a half feet deep was dug, and filled with hardwood coals to a depth of about eight inches. On this hot bed the whole head, hide and all, was laid, and covered with a few more inches of live coals. The hole was then completely filled and rounded over with earth. Cooked in its juices for several hours, the hog's head came from the hole resembling a large lump of charcoal, but the flavor appealed greatly to such epicures of the brush country as usually feasted on it, and doubtless others who like choice, well-prepared meats would have found enjoyment in this frontier treat.

Wild razorback hogs were descendants of a breed that had run wild for centuries in the brush country. They ranged as far north as Arkansas, where acorns were abundant. They were as wild as any creature can be. When a rider came suddenly upon one of those old boars or sows, he had to be on the lookout for a charge.

Riding one day alone in the brush, I startled a little bunch of javalinas, which started trotting over a cow trail leading along a high-cut bank of the Nueces. My horse was one that would not stand quiet while being fired from, so off I jumped, and took a shot at the leading pig, which was running within a foot of the embankment. I must have misjudged his speed, for the bullet I intended for his shoulder struck him in the cheek. He jumped sidewise from the sudden shock, and nothing being under him but the Nueces, down he went into it. The current carried him along rapidly, struggling a little just under water. Snatching up a forked stick, I ran along the bank some distance, and waited for him to come by. When he did, I thrust the stick across his back and held him under water till his struggles ceased, then fished him out, cut off the hams and loin, and returned to camp with good food tied to my saddle.

I did not hunt javalinas at night. In the daytime I sometimes came upon them in large droves, and occasionally I might meet a sow with a litter.

When a drove was encountered, it was well to be alert for trouble. I remember once I decided I would rope one, just for fun, on open ground. I found my opportunity, but things didn't work out quite as I had planned.

When the loop closed on that pig, he gave a squeal that transformed the entire drove into just so many fighting units. Those hogs would charge anything that came into their line of vision. With their two pairs of knife-like tusks pointing both up and down, they would close in on an enemy, spinning around on their hind feet like a circular saw. When those tusks came in contact with a dog, wolf, or horse, they inflicted terrible punishment.

Thinking of this, I slackened my rope, and fortunately for me the pig jumped out of it. I retreated quickly, coiling my reata. The javalinas did not attempt to follow me on their short legs. I have heard stories of men being treed by wild hogs. I never was treed, for I was usually mounted, and if a pig squealed too loudly, summoning help, I generally made for camp.

Dogs were trained to hunt wild hogs. Along about Christmas time, the coolest part of the year in southern Texas, came "hog-killin' time," when the inhabitants planned to lay in a supply of pork. Still-hunting javalinas and razorbacks was a slow process, so dogs were used to bring the wild hogs to bay, and to hold them while the hunters slipped up and shot them, one by one.

As opportunity offered now and then, I would slip out of camp with my rifle and go into the brush. I took great pride in my marksmanship; my early training testing rifles for Alden Brown had made me expert. Ammunition was costly, and I could not afford to use or waste much of it. Making every shot count meant more to me than any speed or fancy juggling of a firearm. If I thought it wasn't possible to place a bullet where it would stop what I fired at, I held my fire. I never hunted with my six-shooter, unless to shoot a cottontail rabbit. It was a wild country, and all I had to do to get game was to prowl around on foot, moving quietly and very slowly, so as not to be seen while I was trying to sight anything moving.

In that thick jungle where we hunted the wild cattle there was danger of attack by Indians at any hour. On these little trips into the brush I never went very far from camp, as I always had Indians on my mind. One might also run into dangerous animals — wolves, Mexican leopards, jaguars, ocelots. It would be an accident, however, if I saw any of the big cats in daytime. They and the ringtailed cats and the armadillos were night prowlers.

Another danger for which one had to keep a sharp lookout was poisonous reptiles and insects. Diamond rattlers found plenty of food and shelter in the patches of cactus, as did other varieties of snakes. One kind, called by the Mexicans the "Frio snake," sometimes grew to a length of seven feet, and its greatest diameter was normally about two inches. These snakes were black, and when they saw that they were observed, they would straighten out to full length and lie perfectly still, so that they looked like straight, burnt sticks. In addition to a plentiful supply of snakes there were centipedes, scorpions, tarantulas, and vinegarroons by the million. With these poisonous pests everywhere, it was necessary to be extremely cautious when picking up wood for the campfire.

On rare occasions, professional jaguar hunters came into camp, accompanied by their packs of dogs. These men were generally ex-Confederate soldiers who had been crippled in the war, and were trying to pick up a little money through the sale of pelts. The skins were sometimes sold to traders who hauled freight over the old wagon trails between San Antonio, then the largest city in Texas, and cities in Mexico. (Main wagon roads ran through the country where I was working, leading to various crossings on the Rio Grande. At these crossings were Mexican settlements which later developed into such towns as Eagle Pass, Laredo, El Paso.)

Sometimes I went with the hunters, if they were hunting near by, so that I didn't have to be away for more than an hour or two. The men had little trailing to do; that was the job of the dogs. If they struck a trail of a big cat, they would follow it until they brought the animal to bay in a cave or up a tree. Often they treed a jaguar, leopard, ocelot, or one of the numerous other wild cats. When the dogs had one of the creatures up a tree, the hunters entered the picture. They seldom carried rifles, but usually had an old cap-and-ball six-shooter. When a hunter shot a big cat out of a tree, he had to act quickly to prevent his dogs from tearing it to pieces before he had obtained its skin. He took the skins to his shack, stretched them, and dried them to make them ready for sale. Those who knew how, tanned the skins and made small rugs of them, for these could be sold for a better price than the raw pelts would bring.

One evening an old man walked into camp just as we were about to have supper, and joined us in a meal of broiled ribs and corn pone. While he was eating I stole a glance at this interesting old fellow. Across his face lay a scar made by a Civil War bullet, which had destroyed one eye. With him was what Texans called a "long-eared hollerin' hound." He and the dog would strike a trail of "el tigre," and when the hound treed the animal, the old man would shoot it down and take its hide. This was only one of his ways of getting pocket money.

One of the cowhands, peering at him closely, asked, "Didn't I see you in Frio Town the other day, riding a little mule, with a game chicken under your arm?"

"Young man," replied the old hunter, "if you saw any kind of chicken with me, you can bet your life it was game."

He was a character, and well known in that part of the country. At times he was employed by sheepmen to herd their flocks. He also owned a racing mule that could run fifty yards and turn a stake faster than many horses. He raised a few fighting chickens at his place on Cibolo Creek. When he ran out of tobacco or other necessities, he went to Frio Town or Dog Town with some jaguar hides, and took a game chicken or two along. There he staged chicken fights and raced his mule as long as he had a dollar with which to transact business. When the sport was over, he would return to his shack and stay there until he could get what he called some more "produce."

XI : OUTLAWS AND REDSKINS

Occasionally I came into contact with detachments of United States cavalry stationed at various military posts along the western border of Texas. Lieutenant Rucker, an officer of the Ninth Regiment, became interested in me, and we began there on the frontier a friendship that lasted through the years.

This officer rode up to the Slaughter ranch one day with a detachment of soldiers on the trail of a band of desperados. He needed a guide and tracker to lead his men to water holes, and to help them locate the renegades, who had vanished into the dense jungle.

It was risky for anyone to give information about outlaws. The soldiers had to depend for guidance on Mexicans, mainly, or on some thoughtless newcomer who had not yet given consideration to the danger involved. Any hunted man who might later ride into the cow camp and sit down for a meal would feel quite justified in putting a bullet through any one of us whom he suspected of having given help to the law.

Unaware of this element in the adventure, I wanted very much to be the one to guide the Lieutenant, and he approached Mr. Slaughter with the request that I be allowed to do it. While they were discussing it, a troop of Texas Rangers commanded by Captain McNally rode into camp, in search of the same band. Consequently, when Mr. Slaughter gave his consent, I set out as guide for both detachments.

One of the Mexicans had told me that he had the day before sighted a bunch of white men mounted on good horses and wearing good clothes. We struck straight for a water hole he named, where I found fresh sign of a camp, and a trail made by several horses, which led toward a larger water hole a few miles farther on. We followed the trail. About a half mile away from the second water hole I dismounted, and leaving my horse with the other riders, set off on foot toward what I thought might be the hideout of the outlaws.

Approaching very cautiously through the chaparral and cactus, I finally caught a glimpse of the men, nearly all lying carelessly about on the ground, and apparently feeling quite safe. I stole back and reported.

When I located the camp my part was done, so I did not accompany the men, but returned to the ranch. I got the rest of the story later from Lieutenant Rucker.

The horses of the two commands were at once placed under guard, and orders were given to surround the encampment at the water hole. No shot was to be fired until orders were given.

The outlaws were surrounded in broad daylight. Rangers and soldiers were able to approach close to the camp under cover of yuccas and big cactus. The desperados were ordered to surrender or be killed, and when they did not obey instantly, the order to fire was given. Twelve of the band were shot down.

That was my first venture in scouting. As I became more conscious of the danger involved, I grew less eager to help. The troops, I reasoned, could dispense with my small store of information and skill, while for my part, I wished to continue wearing my hide for at least a few more years.

Indians also added to the liveliness of life in the brush country. We never knew when we might expect a visit from a little uninvited party of roving Lipans or Comanches. These inconsiderate callers usually dropped in when the moon was at the full, with the unneighborly intention of ambushing us to get our guns, pistols, ammunition, and knives. It was almost the only way they had of obtaining such materials; and while they were about it, they seemed to have no serious objection to riding or driving off our horses. Well-broken horses, trained in capturing wild cattle, were of great value to the Indians in buffalo hunting on the plains farther north.

Another of their not very endearing habits was to slip up near our camp at night and present compliments in the form of a little shower of arrows or lead. This induced us to sleep some distance from the campfire. We would even change our bed-ground two or three times in a night, in order not to be located so easily. A snoring man was an abomination in a cow camp, just as he is now in a sleeping car — but for a very different reason. If we cared at all about the life of a noisy sleeper, we felt that someone must stand guard over him while he snored.

While we were at work with the cattle, Indians had the advantage over us. Only their poor marksmanship with rifle or pistol saved the life of many a cow hunter. If we were fired on while driving a bunch of cattle, about the only chance we had for our lives was to let the cattle go, spur out of range, jump off our horses, and lie flat on the ground, ready for any redskin who dared follow. Or we might dismount immediately, and go still-hunting for Indians. This would put us on more than even terms with them. They learned in time that it was dangerous business to follow anyone who escaped their close-range flight of arrows.

In the days of the muzzle-loading rifles and revolvers, the Indian had the advantage. First he would draw the fire of his enemy, then rush in with bow or lance and try to finish the kill before the white man could reload. Breech-loading rifles

These inconsiderate callers had the unneighborly intention of ambushing us.

and cartridges ended that kind of attack, and long-range guns like the old Sharps carbine added to the red man's fighting problems. After seeing one of his braves killed from a distance of nearly a mile by one of these rifles, one old chief is said to have exclaimed, "Damn white man's guns! Shoot today, kill tomorrow!"

In fighting, the Indian generally used a kind of hit-and-run method. He knew that if not disabled he could attack and get away. Experience taught him that it was wiser to fight a little and run away a great deal. Except in moving pictures I have never seen Indians use mass fighting formations. Every brave tried to leave plenty of room about him. He also took full advantage of the cover afforded by nature. His supplies were always decidedly limited, for no arsenals turned out arrows by the thousand, and no supply trains brought him food or munitions. Each Indian usually made his own arrows, and took care of them. His first thought when not fighting or hunting was for his supply of arrows. Those that were warped he would straighten out either with his teeth or with a tool made from the hump bone of a buffalo.

Indians used various methods of creeping up on a camp of cow hunters, or on a lone rider. A tuft of grass or a yucca plant, aided by a covering of sand on the body, often served to hide the stalkers most effectively. In daytime, to keep their black hair from being spotted by watchful eyes, they would cover it with a piece of buckskin or of brush. They could remain motionless for long periods, like cats. When hunting game or scouting, they never rode or walked on high ridges or made show of themselves on high ground, as white scouts are often depicted as doing, in motion pictures. In their travels the red men used the valley bottoms and kept out of sight.

A wounded Indian was carried or dragged away if possible out of the range of the enemy. Considering the exposure, hunger, and filth of his lodge which were about all the treatment he could look forward to, the recovery of the Indian in certain cases I knew was miraculous. Perhaps it was because the sources of infection had not yet arrived via civilization, or because the maggots always took charge of their wounds.

Extracting deeply imbedded arrows from a wounded man was not an easy operation, as I learned painfully later. When the arrow had been driven in hard, so that the head protruded, the Indians cut the head loose, and pulled out the shaft by its feather end. Such an operation was once performed on Red Cloud, the great war chief of the Ogalalla Sioux. As a young man in a fight with the Pawnees, he received a wound which would have proved fatal to one of less power to resist. An arrow was driven almost through the middle of his body, from front to back, so that the head protruded a couple of inches, and the feather end was still exposed. One of his warriors extracted the arrow, and for three days the young chief lay unconscious; but without medical aid, he recovered.

Troops starting out after marauding Indians were accompanied, whenever possible, by a medical officer with hospital supplies. Indian runners or other couriers were used in communication with other commands in the field, or with the forts on which the troops were based. Few home comforts could be enjoyed, or were expected, by soldiers taking part in such warfare, although there were men who complained when hot coffee was lacking, even near a scene of action. Officers, privates, and teamsters all shared in the hardships incident to the service. It was a difficult task, this bringing of peace to the plains and mountains over which the red men roamed, and many a poor soldier paid for it with his life, or suffered hideous wounds in the battles fought to subdue the Indians on our frontiers.

The brush runners of early Texas had for the most part to take care of their own Indian troubles, until the effective help of the Rangers, and later that of the soldiers, was available to clear away many difficulties. But even with Indian troubles largely settled, there was plenty of hard work ahead, getting longhorns out of the thorny jungles.

XII : LONGHORNS NORTHWARD

I had finally locked horns with Longworth, a fact that created in me a desire to leave the country, or at least his company. The trouble had originated when I unintentionally stampeded a decoy herd with a bunch of wild cattle by running into the herd before I realized where I was. Fortunately we managed to hold the cattle, but Longworth was furious. I could hear him saying all sorts of things about my ancestors, and he said them in two languages.

I did not blame him much, for such a thing would irk any man who was endeavoring to make a success of his work. Feeling very contrite for what I had done, I said nothing. But Longworth was not satisfied with verbal attacks.

I had put my leg up over my horse's neck to remove a thorn which was causing me pain when suddenly the enraged caporal burst through the brush at full speed, headed straight for me, and holding in his hand a dead limb which he had broken from a mesquite tree. Passing within three feet of me, he struck at me with the club, using force enough to have crushed my head if the blow had connected. I ducked, and caught the brunt of it on my shoulders.

Longworth kept on running after passing me, probably thinking I would chase him, and that he might get another whack at me. My first outraged desire was to kill him. Then I pictured what that would mean to me; so putting spurs to my horse, I struck out for camp, thoroughly sick at heart, but seeing nothing else that I could do.

I found a white stranger in camp, preparing some food and coffee for himself. He seemed a decent sort, and right then I needed a friend and advisor. I quickly told him what had happened, and got him to look at my arm and shoulder. As he examined the injury he remarked, "He sure tried to kill you, son."

Expecting Longworth to come after me at any moment, I asked the man what I ought to do if he did.

"Why, son, I'll tell you what I'd do. I'd shoot the top of his damned head off the minute he came in sight."

I thought the matter all over, and then told him what I wanted to do.

"I don't want any killing," I said. "I just want to get square with Longworth. If I could only get him disarmed, I think maybe I could whip him."

This seemed to amuse the stranger. After a moment he said, "I'll tell you what we'll do. I'll put my saddle to one side about forty yards, and lie down and go to sleep. When that hyena comes to camp, you kind of mosey 'round till he puts his gun down. Then you sidle up and baste the soul out of him. If he tries to come any game over you, I'll put a bullet right between his eyes and we'll take a horse and hide out."

"All I want is a fair show to whip Longworth," I said.

"Well, you'll sure git it," was his answer, and somehow I believed he meant it.

I must say that I put in a nervous, unhappy time of it, waiting for the outfit to come in. They had remained in the brush to help pen the cattle. When they did come straggling in, the caporal was in the lead, whistling — a thing I had never known him to do before. He rode into camp taking no notice of me, jumped from his horse, pulled his rifle from his saddle, and leaned it against a tree. Then he unsaddled his horse and turned it loose. To my surprise, he also unbuckled his belt, throwing it with his pistol and knife down on the saddle. Walking over to me, he asked, "Supper ready?"

"You'll take a licking before you ever eat again, you cowardly cur," I shouted, and accompanied the remark with a good slap on his jaw.

"Why, boy, I don't want any trouble with you," he laughed. "I admit I was a little rattled when you stampeded the cattle, but I wouldn't hurt you for anything."

I noticed that he had an eye on the stranger. He had seen his saddle horse near the camp when riding in, and that, I think, was the cause of his whistling and good humor. I thought I could see why he wasn't looking for trouble with me just then.

As the Mexicans had all seen me slap our caporal, I thought I had done enough, so I answered, "We'll call the matter settled, then."

And there it rested. As soon as he could do so without attracting attention, Longworth curled up for a rest close to his weapons.

Even then, however, although there may have been no occasion for it, I was still wary of Longworth: I wanted to leave him. This incident illustrates the small value placed on human life in that neck of the woods. Every man felt that he had the power of judge, jury, and executioner. If it meant saving his own bacon, hardly a ruffian hesitated to exercise those powers. To live in the brush country one had to take such chances with life.

I had learned the brush-running game thoroughly, in all its difficulties and dangers. I had learned by experience what it meant to get pretty well warmed up chasing wild longhorns and branding them under southern skies. I knew well enough what a Texas "norther" could do to the marrow. I had made trips for supplies to Laredo and to Corpus Christi. So I felt I knew a lot about Texas.

A region I longed to know better was the vast buffalo country lying between the heads of the Nueces and Frio rivers and Kansas. My opportunity to realize this desire soon came. The cattle I had helped to gather and put into Slaughter's pastures were to be driven northward to the Kansas markets. Herds would be started on the trail about the first of March. I went to Charlie Slaughter, who was to superintend the marketing of the first herd of cattle, and asked him if I might go up the trail with the herd.

"Why, boy," he replied, "the Yankees up there might kill you off. You'd better stay here, and ketch mavericks."

I promised him that if he would let me go I would return when the cattle were sold, and chase mavericks for him. At that he replied, "Well, then, let's go and see Joe about it."

Joe Roberts, who had been selected from among the Slaughter employees to take charge of the first or lead herd in the big drive, looked me over, and said, "They tell us you can catch a cow, and can shoot a rabbit's eye out every pop. Now if you can ride for the next four months without a whole night's sleep, and turn your gun loose on any damned Injun that tries to get our horses, well, get ready. We roll out tomorrow."

I broke all records, getting my personal belongings moved over to his camp.

A new experience was ahead for me, helping to take a herd of longhorns northward over the cattle trails. I was to have my part in the business which did so much for the development of the West — the expansion to reach the great eastern markets which were beginning to demand longhorn beef, and the ranches that were springing up over the great northern plains.

It had been demonstrated not only that these wild cattle could be fattened on the nutritious grasses of the buffalo ranges; they could, if they were in good flesh in the fall, withstand the rigors of the northern winters. As a result cattle ranching grew swiftly into an attractively profitable business which brought new vitality to the West, and spotted the grazing grounds between Texas and the Canadian border with thriving ranches. The Lone Star State now had a market for all the longhorns it could supply.

The driving of hundreds of thousands of these native cattle northward began in earnest. Year after year, new trails were marked out. These followed mainly the old lines of march of the buffalo migrations to the rich grazing grounds of the North in the spring and back in the fall to their winter pastures under sunnier skies.

Men in charge of driving and marketing at first took not only cattle bearing their own brands, but also other cattle they might gather, regardless of brand. A record was supposed to be kept by those in charge of the cattle belonging to the various ranchmen, and after the expense of marketing was deducted, the proceeds of the sales were supposed to be turned back to the respective owners. In some cases these proceeds failed to materialize. Later on a system of inspection of herds at different points on the trail before the cattle left Texas put a stop to at least some of the loose business methods that prevailed during the earlier drives.

When Ben Slaughter and his sons had gathered enough cattle to start some herds to market and the time had come for the drive to begin, there was a rounding up of the herds in the big pastures. For months the cow catchers in their different camps had worked gathering cattle over a large area extending from the forks to the heads of the Nueces and the Frio, and as far toward the Rio Grande as the old Cotulea rancho, midway between San Antonio and Laredo. The range over which I had hunted the wild longhorns was about a hundred miles square.

The cattle we had captured had been turned into the large pastures. Each enclosure would take in an area equal to two or three townships. When they were built, many wild cattle were fenced in, and the other cattle turned loose with them soon became as wild as the wildest. It was not an easy task to round up such a herd, even within the big pastures; but with our large outfit of skilled riders, we soon had a herd of twenty-five hundred thrown together.

These were driven into the stoutly built corrals to have a road brand put on them. Getting a hot iron on their hides took real skill. They could kick as actively as a horse. If they could only knock a man down and kick him a time or two for good measure as he fell, they would try to finish the job by jumping on him with their forefeet, hooking him while snorting a vigorous message in his ear.

We left till the last, for some wild fun, any strong yearling bulls among the cattle to be branded, so that we could stage a bull fight with them when the branding was done. There were men among each crew of cow hunters who dared to go on foot into the corral with one of those spike-horned bulls when it was enraged. Using a saddle blanket to keep the vicious animal from locating him, the amateur matador would have a lively time with the snorting bull, while the rest of us enjoyed the dangerous sport.

At last, the roundup completed, the branding done, the trail outfit ready, we let down the pasture bars and pointed the big herd of longhorns northward.

XIII : START — AND STAMPEDE!

Men trained in trailing cattle through the brush country were in demand for the great drives over the old Chisholm and other cattle routes. All the skill that could be mustered was needed to guide big herds of two to four thousand head over a thousand miles or more of open country, to shipping points on the railroad, or to the ranches of the northern plains.

Brush runners' experience made them invaluable in this work. To drive a decoy herd to a place where it could be held while wild cattle were circled and run into it required cowboy skill of a high order. The point rider who acted as leader of the decoy herd, singing as he rode so that other riders could follow him with the cattle, had to possess a sixth sense in order to find his way back and forth with the herd in country which looked the same in every direction. It also took skill on the part of the other riders to keep the herd moving in the direction of the singing rider.

On the open plains two point drivers, one on either side of the leaders, were assigned to give direction to the herd. Swing drivers in pairs on opposite sides of the herd held the cattle in line and kept them trailing after the leaders. Still other cowboys acted as a rear guard to bring up the drag end of the herd. Back and forth at a little distance from the long line of cattle the swing drivers would ride, keeping the longhorns moving ever northward.

Taking those great herds to market was a serious business, involving large sums of money, and was in no wise a Wild West show. Riders engaged in the work were not at all showy in dress or in equipment. Trail herders for the most part were armed with six-shooters and sheath knives; rifles were carried in the mess wagon for Indian raids and other emergencies. There were real dangers to be faced along the trail.

The country through which the herds were trailed was wide open. No barbed-wire fences then existed between the Gulf of Mexico and the Canadian border. Neither were there any settlements, other than an occasional military post, over that vast stretch. Bridges had not yet been built across the streams which wandered over the plains, rising with the rains or melting snows, and falling during the dry seasons until many of them disappeared, at times, in their sandy beds.

Much has been written about the conflicts that developed between the cattlemen, who first used these plains, and those who came to settle. When the pioneer farmers came, naturally they began to turn the sod over which the buffalo had roamed, and to fence off claims within the range country; but during nearly seventy years of association with cowboys and ranchers of the West, I never found one who would not share his last crust with any honest settler. Probably there were mean, grasping cattlemen, just as there were unpleasant men engaged in other occupations, but I was never thrown among them. The old life in the good open country tended to expand the heart and promote a kindly feeling for mankind.

On starting a herd north, the caporal would order his point drivers to keep the cattle headed ever toward Kansas, guided by some landmark he would indicate, if one could be seen. Then he would ride ahead, perhaps for miles, to look for a good watering or camping place. We would keep a sharp lookout for his return and the signal he might give with his hat from a mile or more away, for us to follow him, or to throw the herd off the trail to graze. It was only when they wanted to stop the cattle to graze that the point drivers would ride in close to the head of the herd. Given the signal, they would ride ahead and check the leaders, and let the rest of the herd close up. In a short time the hungry herd would be grazing. When satisfied, the cattle would lie down to rest until the riders strung them out again for another lap of the long drive.

Taking those great herds to market was a serious business involving large sums, and was in no wise a Wild West show.

Roberts had in his trail crew twelve riders and a cook. The cook drove two yoke of oxen hitched to our canvas-covered supply wagon. We were most fortunate on that trip in having one of the best cooks and drivers that ever popped a bull whip on a cattle trail — Old John, we called him.

Much praise must be given to the best of those old-time trail cooks. Men who performed this important work usually were veterans of the frontier. A camp cook could do more than any other man in the outfit to make life pleasant for everybody on those hard drives. If he was good-natured and hustling, he was a boon to the boss as well as to the cowboys. A cheery voice ringing clear about daybreak, "Roll out, there, fellers, and hear the little birdies sing their praises to God," or "Arise and shine, and give God the glory!" would make the most crusty cow waddie grin — even when he was half dead for want of sleep — as he crawled from his blanket to eat his breakfast.

On the morning of our start up the trail all was in readiness. For this trip I was given the best five of the saddle horses I had been riding in the brush. Each of us was allowed to take a pair of bed blankets and a sack containing a little extra clothing. No more load than was considered absolutely essential was permitted in the wagon, for there would be no wagon road over most of the country we were to traverse, and there was plenty of rough country with steep-banked rivers to be crossed. We had no tent or shelter of any sort but our blankets. Our food and cooking utensils were the same as those we had used in the cow camps of the brush country.

There was no provision for caring for the men in case of sickness or accident. Should anyone be injured or wounded, or seized with illness, he would be strictly out of luck. Quick recovery or sudden death were the only desirable alternatives in such case, for much of the time the outfit would be far from settlements and medical or surgical aid. No painting or word picture of the life of the early cowboy has represented, nor could it represent, many of the hardships and dangers which attended those who constantly, day and night, rode with the herd. Their chief shelter was their own weatherbeaten skin. Yet despite all rigors of the trail and its many dangers, these heroic men were marked by loyalty to their work. They stayed with the herd, despite all hazards.

Most of the men selected for this first northward drive were white. The few Mexican vaqueros in the crew were known to be good hands with cattle. A dozen or so extra brush poppers went along for a few days to help break in the longhorns to trailing and to being held by riders day and night — for there would be no more corrals — and also to assist us until we got out of the brush country to the open plains. This done, they turned back to give help to other herds to follow.

On the first day I was told to help drive the saddle horses. My instructions were to keep them following the wagon, which went ahead of the cattle. Behind us along the trail we made came the strung-out herd of longhorns. Roberts pointed out the course he wanted the outfit to take, and then rode on to select our first camp. A few miles ahead he found a place with water and fairly open ground where the cattle could be bedded down for the night. Returning, he told us where to go and where the wagon was to be placed so that it might not be too close to the herd.

Reaching the assigned spot, John unyoked and hobbled his oxen and turned them out to graze. He then began to prepare our supper of cornbread, boiled meat, and coffee. Along toward night about half the men who had been driving cattle came in and ate. Then they caught fresh horses from the band, and returned to the herd, allowing their companions to come in. After these men had eaten, they also caught and saddled fresh mounts, helped to hobble all the horses that were left in the band, and rode off again to the cattle.

Roberts ordered me to catch the gentlest horse in my string and ride out to assist in bedding down the herd, by this time not more than a quarter of a mile away. The bed ground selected by the caporal was about ten acres in extent and had very little brush on it, though the growth was heavy all around. Into this more open space the longhorns were driven at dusk by riders who closed in on all sides, crowding the cattle until they were in a compact bunch. The men began to ride slowly around the herd, a little distance away from it, singing all the while that wordless Texas Lullaby, a tune that went something like this:

I shall long remember that night. The moon was new, and it was not really dark until after ten. None of the cattle had lain down, but they had stopped moving about and were all very quiet, with the exception of one old black cow which had at some time probably been used as a milch cow by a Mexican family, and insisted on feeding through the entire evening. Every rider had sooner or later to turn her back into the herd; for the moment she was left, she would walk away from the other cattle and begin again to graze.

I heard many uncomplimentary remarks in both Spanish and English addressed to that cow during the evening. Perhaps I was rude to her myself, for I had to turn her back into the herd several times.

At last she walked away from the herd about thirty yards and dropped down to rest, to our great relief. We allowed her to lie where she was, changing our course so as to include her in the circle we were riding. She would let us pass within a few feet of her, and never move. Every time I came around I would see how close I could ride to that troublesome old black cow. Like many another boy, I felt the need of an additional outlet for my energy. Finally she allowed me to ride within two feet of her without stirring. By this time the night had grown pitch dark.

The next time around I decided to see if the old longhorn bossy would let me touch her. Riding in as close as possible, I leaned over on one side and touched her neck with my foot. She must have been asleep, for she gave a snort and a bound, and plunged into the herd — or rather, the place where the herd had been; for the instant she snorted, there came a roar and a crash such as I had never heard before, and the earth seemed fairly to tremble. Before she could get among the other longhorns, they were somewhere else. The herd had stampeded!

Not knowing what else to do, I dashed along in the direction in which the cattle had disappeared. Once in a while I could hear coming from the brush the yells of our hard-riding men. I wandered about for a time, until at last I blundered into one of the Mexicans.

"What's the matter?" I asked.

"The herd has stampeded," he replied. "We won't have one of them by morning."

"What stampeded them?" I asked, cautiously.

"Diòs sabe." ("God knows.")

I devoutly hoped that no one else did.

The entire herd did not get away, for fortunately the scared longhorns stuck pretty well together, and ran in the direction of one of the large pasture fences. Some of the boys stayed with them, and managed to hold most of the bunch along the fence till daylight, when all of us got after them and brought them back to camp. When the herd was strung out and tallied, we found we were short about five hundred head.

"We'll take what we have left of this herd and get right out of the brush country," said Roberts, "and then wait for enough more to make up the difference." So we rolled away once more.

No one knew what had started those cattle, and unless some of the men who were there are still living, and happen to read this, it will not matter that I have come clean at last! I kept very mum. One of the cowboys got hurt rather badly by running into a limb, and two others were dismounted when their horses stepped into holes or tripped over fallen brush. My experience in trying to find out just how gentle that old black cow was proved a tremendous success, although doubtless it cost a little money. My employer's loss was my gain, for I had learned my lesson, and I never again tried such an experiment.

For some time we had no more stampedes. After the first night, we divided the night herding into two watches, half the outfit being on guard at a time. When we were clear of the brush country the extra men turned back, and as the cattle were now pretty well broken to being night-herded, we divided the watch into three tricks, three men going on guard at a time with the cattle, and one with the horses.

Each night all the horses were hobbled, but they had to be herded just the same, for they would stampede at night just as cattle would. Everything depended upon our holding our saddle horses.

When the extra men turned back to the ranch we lay over for a few days until Allen Harris, another of Slaughter's foremen, came up with another herd of a few hundred head to replace the cattle we had lost. We cut out these extra cattle. Then, keeping the two herds a few miles apart, we started along the old Chisholm Trail.

XIV : COMANCHES

Indian sign was seen daily, but we had no trouble with the redskins until after we had left the head of the Frio River and started for Painted Rocks. Then one night the Indians attempted to stampede the Harris herd by running into it on their ponies, dragging a buffalo robe at the end of a rope. Both cattle and horses took fright and broke into a wild run, but the men stayed with the stock and held them.

It was the Comanches who were hovering along our trail performing this deviltry. They were a pretty venturesome bunch, and they must have got quite a lot of excitement and fun from the trouble they caused us. Once or twice they slipped up close to the herd at night and shot a longhorn or two with their arrows. When thus struck an animal would bawl with pain and plunge around, causing a stampede of more or less magnitude, besides supplying the Indians with some meat.

We were on the lookout for Indians all the time.

Every one of us expected to get an arrow while riding around the stock at night. It was a great relief for all when each day broke, for we felt that it gave us at least half a show for our lives.

One night we were camped on a creek that ran into the Llano River, near its head. Throughout that day we had seen a good many fresh Indian signs. I was on first watch with the horses; Roberts had assigned me to that duty for both early evening and the hours before daybreak. These were the favorite times for the Indians to perform. I was known to be the best shot in the outfit, and it was expected that I would score straight bull's-eyes and not get buck fever, no matter how numerous, hideous, or dangerously close the human targets.

==The country was rough, with here and there large cedar brakes.== I held the horses pretty close to the wagon after supper, and everyone noticed that they were very restless. For some reason, in those days a white man's horse was afraid of the sight or smell of an Indian, just as Indian ponies were afraid of white men. When our animals scented redskins, they sniffed, snorted, ran together, and showed terror in appearance as well as action.

Then Roberts ordered me to put the herd in a little opening in the middle of the big cedar brake near the wagon. I told him that I was afraid to go in there to herd, as the Indians could slip up close in the thicket and kill me with an arrow without being seen. Roberts argued that there would be a great deal less danger in the brakes than on the open prairie, where red thieves were likely to run between the herd and the wagon, and not only kill me, but get away with the horses. "They can't run their ponies in that brake," he concluded. So into the cedars we went, the caporal assisting me to drive the animals. After putting me on this dangerous spot and cautioning me to keep a sharp lookout, Roberts returned to camp.

It required all the nerve I possessed to remain there with the horses. My job was to keep circling them, to hold the nervous animals within as small a space as possible. I had to ride hard to keep them within the area, for they kept snorting and trying to scatter. When riding on the side of the herd nearest camp, I was about seventy-five yards from the wagon.

After what seemed an age, I heard one of the boys from the cattle herd ride into camp to arouse the men of the next watch.

The night was dark and chilly. One of the boys had put a lot of dry wood on the campfire, so that I could see the men around it quite plainly. It did not take them long to get out, for all hands slept with their clothes on, and every rider kept his horse close by, saddled and ready for emergencies all night.

Frank Dennis, one of the old-school cowboys, and as brave a man as ever lived, was to relieve me. I started toward camp when I saw Frank coming. He had thrown his bed blanket over his shoulders, Indian fashion, in place of an overcoat. As I passed him I said, "Frank, you'll have to ride hard to hold the horses."

He told me he was blinded from having been so long in the light of the campfire, so I rode back with him to go around the horses once or twice. At last he said, "All right, Jim, I can see 'em now, and I'll set 'em a while."

With that I started for camp again, and riding up to the campfire, I swung down from my horse, rifle in hand; for I had been carrying it, ready to shoot, all evening. As my foot touched the ground, I heard about two dozen shots in quick succession. Turning my head, I could see flashes from guns, and I took a shot in the direction of the flashes. My horse, which had turned his head too when the shots first came, got an Indian bullet squarely in his forehead, and went down at my feet, dead.

I jumped away from that campfire fast, and crawled under a big cedar tree, the branches of which came very close to the ground. Every man had run for his life into the thicket. Soon our horse herd came tearing right through camp. Running against the ropes we had stretched from the wagon wheels to make a corral, the frightened animals upset the wagon. Before the firing began some daring Indian had slipped into camp, cut the picket rope of one horse, and led it away. All the rest of the horses saddled and picketed about camp ran on their ropes, broke them, and decamped with the rest of the stampeded herd.

Plunging into the cattle, the horse herd set the longhorns stampeding into the big cedar brake. The crashing and crackling of brush and branches under the hoofs of that crazed mass of animals made about as great an uproar as any cowboy ever heard. The men with the cattle did not dare yell at the animals or sing to them, lest the Indians locate and slip an arrow into somebody.

I lay quite still under the tree. After a time I heard Roberts' voice calling out, "Don't let 'em get away with the horses, boys! Stay with 'em! Come on, boys, where are you?"

I don't know where the caporal disappeared to when the horses stampeded through camp, but he certainly went somewhere for a few minutes. I don't see, either, how he expected us, on foot, to hold the horse herd. One by one I could hear the boys answering him. I didn't like to get out from beneath that tree; but neither did I care to be called a coward, so I joined him, although I thought it the most foolish thing we could possibly do. It was so dark that an Indian could have slipped up within three feet without being seen.

Frank Dennis did not appear, and I made up my mind he had been killed. "Let's go and see if we can find Frank," I said to Roberts. "I know where he was riding, and I saw the shooting." We searched, but failed to find any trace of him. We wandered here and there until daybreak.

By that time the men who had been with the cattle came in, bringing some of our horses. They had managed to hold the herd, which they said was about half a mile from camp. I had my saddle, but several of the other saddles were gone. I gave mine to the caporal, and joined other boys riding bareback, the order of the day for some.

About sunrise Frank Dennis rode into camp, a little pale, but quite cheerful.

"Well, fellers, good mornin'," he said. "Pleasant night, wasn't it?" When he swung down from his horse, I saw that he had blood on his clothes, and that his hand was tied up with a bloody handkerchief. He told us his story.

After I left him he had ridden around the herd a time or two. A large band of Indians had crawled up to within about fifteen feet of the circle he was riding, and as he passed they blazed away at him. He was so close I suppose they thought they couldn't help getting him, and they probably counted on their shooting to stampede the horses, as well. They would then have run to their own horses, tied close at hand, mounted, and driven off our stampeded animals.

But their plan did not work very well. They succeeded only in shooting a hole through the center of Frank's hand, and in giving him two or three slight flesh wounds. In addition he had about a dozen holes through his blanket and saddle, and one shot tore off his saddle horn. An arrow lodged between his saddle and blanket.

The horse herd scattered after passing camp. Some ran into the cattle herd, where they were held by the boys with the longhorns. One bunch was chased by the Indians up a canyon, but the horses were unable to get out because of the vertical walls, and the redskins were afraid to drive them back down the gorge, and so they had to let them go. As it was, the savages got away with about a quarter of our mounts.

In the middle of that afternoon two buffalo hunters came into our camp on foot, and reported that the Comanches had just run off their whole bunch of ten horses. They wanted to borrow some ponies from us so that they might follow the thieves and try to regain their stock. Roberts did not like to spare the horses, but he did let them take two, and said, "If any of you boys want to go with these men for a day or two to see if you can get back some of our horses, why, go ahead."

I for one was ready. I was tired of being hunted, and wanted to do some hunting myself. Two other boys were of the same mind, so the three of us were allowed to accompany the hunters. First we went to their camp and took the trail of their horses, for we were sure all the captured animals would be thrown together. Some of their horses were shod, and could be more easily trailed than ours.

Evidently the Indians did not consider us capable of following them, for after making off not more than twenty miles they went into camp.

We located them the first evening out, and crawled up as close as we could. Their camp was by a spring in some willow brush. It was in a small valley — almost a canyon, surrounded by hills on three sides. Three of us went to the brow of a hill to overlook the camp from one side of the valley, while the buffalo hunters took their position on the other side. We hid our horses in another small valley behind us.

This band of Comanches was doubtless striking for old Mexico, for those we found in camp — fourteen in all, as I recollect it — were nearly all old men and old women. The stolen stock had been left with these older ones to be taken to a safe place, while the younger men and squaws took another spin around to see what further plunder they might accumulate. We saw that they had some horses picketed to willows about the edge of the thicket, and ours were among them.

We waited for daylight. Not only did we want those horses; we were all wild to get a shot at an Indian.

As it began to grow light we could see a stir in the camp. Presently one old Indian came out of his tepee and started to walk to the top of the hill behind their camp. One of our boys, Bell, who was lying about fifty yards from me, could stand the strain no longer. Drawing a fine bead, he blazed away at the old buck, striking him in the middle of his body. In another second, bucks and squaws were running about in all directions.

The hunters now opened fire with their buffalo guns, and some of the Indians started our way on foot.

One redskin, leaping on a pony, came charging up the hill straight toward where I was lying. He rode flattened out, hitting the little horse at every jump with a rawhide rope, one end of which was fastened about the pony's jaw. One of the hunters began firing on this Indian, making me lie low, for his bullets were striking closer to my hiding place than to the running target. When the redskin came within a short distance he suddenly swerved to pass me. Not daring to rise up to a proper shooting position out of the buffalo wallow where I lay, I merely took a pot shot at him as he passed. My bullet broke his pony's back just behind the rider's seat. The pony went down, but the Indian went over its head, landed on his feet, and continued his flight. He dashed into a bunch of willows in a little valley behind me, causing me extreme mental discomfort, for he had had a gun in his hand when he passed.

Those Indians that had not been shot were now speeding down the valley. I ran to their camp, yelling to the boys not to shoot at me, and cut a lot of the horses loose from the willows. Among them was the night horse which had been stolen from our camp before the Indians fired on Frank Dennis. The saddle was still on its back. Other horses were hobbling about in every

Not daring to rise up to a proper shooting position, I took a pot shot at him as he passed.

direction. I jumped on to the saddled animal and soon rounded them up.

All of us got together then and drove the entire bunch, Indian ponies and all, to the spot where our own animals were tied. We took some of the Indian saddles and blankets which had been left behind, for we knew that squaw saddles were better than none, and it was quite a distance to the nearest place where cowboy saddles could be purchased.

About fifteen head of Indian ponies had been captured. With these and our own recaptured animals, including nearly all of those lost by the hunters, we lit out for camp and the cattle herd.

We all felt that our best move would be to get out of that country as fast as possible, and so we set out on the long trail once more. Frank Dennis was the only one of us brave enough to laugh at the adventure. Nearly every day while dressing his wounded hand, he would chuckle and say, "You sure taught those red devils to take a joke." But I thought we had taught a band of Indians what white men could and would do when driven to it. We had no more trouble with redskins on that trip; and there were no more stampedes for some time.

XV : TRICKS AND TROUBLES

In our outfit was a man named Jack Harris — a large, hungry looking fellow of forty, with a war record, I have no doubt. He had been having fun at my expense all along the trail. Every chance he could get he would ride up to me, suddenly draw his six-shooter, cock it, and aim it at me, saying, "Are you the sheriff that is looking for me?"

Generally he would wind up this little act by taking his revolver by the barrel, his finger on the trigger guard, and reaching the butt toward me, and saying, "I'm tired of fighting; take my gun." Allowing some imaginary sheriff time to reach for it, he would reverse the weapon quick as a flash, cock it again, and aim straight for my face. All this, he said, was "just for practice." I think it was, for later I found out that he could be a bad man in some places.

One day before we reached Fort Griffin, he played his gun game on me once more. After he had put up his revolver, I said, "Jack, don't practice on me any more."

"Why not?"

"Because it would be dangerous for you," I replied. "If this sort of thing goes on, it will be only a matter of time before you will let your thumb slip, and I might go dead. Then you'd be sorry. I would rather be killed purposely than by accident. If you ever aim a gun at me again, you'd better shoot, for I will surely kill you if I can."

He rode away and did not speak to me again for several days. Meanwhile, we arrived at Fort Griffin, a frontier army post comprising officers' quarters, barracks, and a large sutler's store, all built of adobe. An Indian camp of Tonkaway scouts and trailers employed by the army was stationed near by. Many thousands of buffalo hides were brought in to Fort Griffin from hunters' camps, and stacked there until freighters from Fort Worth could haul them to the railroad.

While at the fort we took on a fresh stock of provisions, and all hands had a chance to see the post and secure clothing, tobacco, cartridges, and much-needed saddles at the sutler's store. When his turn came, Jack went to do his buying. While in the store he accidentally left his quirt, and did not miss it until he returned to camp. Since he was not on first watch, he said he would go back during the evening for his quirt.

When the time came for him to go I was on

guard with the horses. Roberts had warned me to keep an eye out for the Tonkaways near the fort, who were not above attempting to steal some of the animals. Then too, loafing about the post were several white horse thieves and a few other noted characters who would slip away with our mounts if they could. I was holding the herd close to camp, and the night was quite dark.

I happened to be near the wagon when Harris was leaving, and I could hear him say, "Boys, I have a notion when I come back to slip up on Jim and fire a shot close to him. I can scare him out of ten years' growth." None of the men commented. He rode off.

I determined to give Harris a red hot reception if he tried any such trick on me. I put the horse herd between camp and the fort, and waited for him. He reappeared in about an hour, but seemed to have changed his mind about the scare he was going to give me, for I could hear him whistling and singing as he approached camp. The nearer he came, the more noise he made. Suddenly he was among the horses before he knew it, and began shouting, "Oh, Jim."

I slipped off my horse and kept quiet. Harris would ride a few feet and then stop and call my name. In this manner he worked his way through the herd almost into camp, where he found all the boys laughing heartily at him. I had followed to hear what was said. When he had picketed his horse, one of the boys remarked, "What was the matter out there? You seemed to want Jim awful bad."

"Yes," said Harris, "and that little devil is out there asleep somewhere, and if something was to wake him up sudden, he's just fool enough to shoot without asking questions."

"That's about the size of it," I heard Roberts say. "And any little ideas you may have in the way of Indian scares for Jim you'd better forget about."

In the morning at breakfast Jack asked, "Where were you last night when I came back?"

"I was on guard with the horses, loaded for anything dangerous that might come along."

"Well, son," he returned, "I won't bother you any more, and we'll be friends." And from that time on till the end of the trip we got along fine.

There were plenty of larger troubles in store for us. During that first year I was on the trail, every river from the Red to the Arkansas was "big swimming." We were fortunate in having no serious accidents to our men while crossing swollen streams, but we lost a number of cattle and horses by drowning.

Bad thunder and hail storms added difficulty. At times we went for days with scarcely a wink of sleep because of winds and rain which made the cattle hard to control. In some places on the trail the ground was boggy from long spells of rain, and we had to resort to all kinds of schemes to snatch a little sleep as opportunity permitted. When three riders were free at a time, they would go a little distance from the cattle, dismount, and lie down in the form of a triangle, each man using his neighbor's ankles for a pillow to keep his head out of the mud and water.

It was easy to drift into sleep, jogging around the herd. There was a limit to the endurance of even a toughened cowboy. My method of combating sleepiness was to mix chewing tobacco with saliva and rub it on my eyelids. This is great treatment when one's thoughts seem all bent on having a nap. It could be called a rouser, but I wouldn't advise employing it if gentler methods are at hand. We had to keep awake, with one eye and one ear open even when we were trying to sleep about those great herds. At any moment, should the herd suddenly stampede in his direction, the cowboy would have to spring into the saddle and ride hard; if it ran in any other direction, he must hear the rumble of horns and hoofs and dash toward the sound, or he would not locate the herd in time to be of any use that night.

It is easy to understand how men of spirit, fired by patriotism in time of war, are willing to endure the privations and sufferings which are a part of military life, but what the spirit was that sustained the early cowboy is more than I can explain. I remember few, and I believe there were few, who proved to be quitters. Above all else in the mind of the cowboy ran the thought, "Stay with the cattle; hold the herd."

None of those who settled our frontiers — cattleman, farmer, soldier — lived a life free from rough work and bitter hardship and loneliness. But I think the wild and woolly cow waddie received as many rough knocks as anybody who ever played a part in the pioneering on the sunset side of the Mississippi. To stay with the cattle and horses during the storms, the cowboy had to ride at breakneck speed, sometimes in darkness so impenetrable that the rider could not see his horse's head. The only relief from such blackness was the blinding flash of lightning that would follow, at times actually playing on the horns of the cattle and on the ears of the horses. It would take days to separate herds camped near one another and hopelessly mixed during a stampede. Many a morning some poor old leather-breeches would come dragging himself into camp, his saddle on his back, and his bones broken. And a few of the boys who had gone down with their horses in those terrible runs had to be left beside the trail to await the trumpeter Gabriel.

When weather was bad we had scarcely enough to eat. Buffalo chips, our only fuel on the prairie, would become so soaked with rain during days of storm that we could not get enough dry ones to make a little coffee, let alone bake bread. But when the weather was fine we had plenty of rest and food, and it was then that I thoroughly enjoyed cowboy life, and would not have exchanged places with a king.

I killed plenty of game along the way. Deer and wild turkeys were plentiful in the blackjack oak country. Antelope and buffalo preferred open ground. I got all we needed of these kinds of game to help out our food supply, and had good sport doing it.

On warm moonlit nights as I rode around the herd I would say to myself, "This is the life!" My horse seemed to understand my thoughts, and to share my feeling. I always picked the best horse in my string for my night animal, and used him whenever I had to night-herd. He and I became real friends. When I was in a merry mood he seemed to feel the same way, and on dark and stormy nights when the cattle were ready to jump and stampede at any minute and everyone was keyed up, I could feel him trembling under me; occasionally when we stood still I could hear his heart thumping with excitement.

About the middle of that summer of 1874 we arrived at Abilene, Kansas, a lively shipping point on the railroad which was being extended across the plains to Denver. Here the cattle, and such horses as were not needed for the return trip, were readily sold to northern buyers. "Us boys" were mighty glad to get a chance for a whole night's sleep. Then after a few days of rest for ourselves and our horses, we struck back over the Chisholm Trail, by way of Fort Worth and San Antonio, to take up again the work of gathering longhorns for the market.

I never crossed Longworth's path again, although probably he was still a working caporal somewhere in the brush country. The memories I carried of him were not pleasant, but I had learned under his leadership the technique of handling wild cattle.

Just after Christmas that year I was on a cow hunt, and we were driving wild cattle into a corral, when suddenly shots were fired near our caporal, who was riding ahead of us, as usual. Back he came right into the herd, yelling, "Indians! Look out, boys!"

Turning my horse, I started to dash for a catclaw thicket close by when a bullet from behind and a little to one side struck my horse just behind the ear, dropping him instantly from full speed. I was thrown over his head with great force, striking my head on the trunk of a big tree. I remember seeing a display of fireworks, and then hearing a voice call out, "Are you hurt, Jim?"

Gun in hand — for automatically I had jerked it from its scabbard — I was trying to stagger to my feet. Someone shouted, "Get down, and lie low!"

I did. Presently, when I recovered and looked about me, I saw some of the men who had been with the herd. One had run his horse into a thicket, jumped off, and dropped down to fight for his life. He told me that when I struck the tree close to where he lay, I had risen to my knees, crawled forward a few feet, and risen to my feet. Luckily the Indians did not follow us into that thicket. We neither saw nor heard from the devils further that day.

Our entire bunch of cattle was scattered and lost. My back was so badly injured by the fall that it was a long time before I could ride with any comfort. Having no one to go to for sympathy, I could only figure that the hair of the dog is good for the bite, and keep going. I have certainly had opportunity to prove to my satisfaction that a person who is young and joyously robust can stand some pretty hard knocks and still make a quick recovery. I would not advise the kind of header I took from that horse, however, for I am sure it would not take many of them to wear out even a tough youngster.

That winter the Indians seemed more active than usual. Not long after my horse was killed under me, we were again waylaid in the brush. This time I did not fare even so well as when I took my fall. I happened to get pretty close to one Indian, and as I whirled my horse around at the first sound of shooting, the lurking redskin drove a dogwood arrow into the calf of my leg. I waited for no more, but took that one to camp as fast as my horse could travel. As I had several miles to ride through cactus and brush and did not know when I might run into more Indians, I put in some miserable moments on that trip.

Reaching camp, I found some of the stampeded riders there, and they helped me from my horse and soon extracted the arrow by main force, hold-

As I whirled my horse the lurking redskin drove a dogwood arrow into my leg.

ing me during the process. The arrow had been driven through my heavy chaps and boot top, into the muscles and cords of my leg. To cut away the legging and boot top about the arrow was a small matter; but probably I was sorry that I had run off with that poor Indian's arrow, for I cried while my Mexican friends took the shaft from my leg. I had a chill, too, when the thought struck me that the arrow might have been poisoned. I had heard many tales of Lipans who had poisoned their war arrows. The Mexicans split some cactus leaves, burned the thorns off, and bound the leaves on my leg, after inserting pepper berries in the wound.

I worried so much about poison that I decided to strike out for San Antonio to find a doctor. Shock, worry, and pain made me dizzy and sick during that long ride. I found the best surgeon in San Antonio, who gave me treatment and soon had me braced up. I remember his saying, "Why, boy, anyone who has lived the life you do, and has no bad habits, couldn't be killed with an ax." In a couple of weeks he approved of my going back to camp, provided I would follow his directions in dressing the wound. My return trip was made shorter by the lightness of my heart. I was soon crashing my way through the brush again, after the wild longhorns.

XVI : MUSTANGS

Mexicans gave the wild horses their name, mustang. Beautiful little creatures they were — generally cream, buckskin, or mouse-colored. A few black marks about the legs above the knees or hocks, and a black stripe along the middle of the back from mane to tail, were common markings. Their average weight was about eight hundred pounds. The stallions did not appear to be shaggy; although they had unusually heavy manes, as a rule they were clean-limbed, and their hoofs were black and perfect. No blacksmith or hoof-shaper had ever tinkered with their feet or forced them to wear iron shoes, and their hoofs would stand wear over the roughest trails. They required no grain, but rustled food for themselves.

It seems certain that these horses were the descendants of the animals brought from Mexico by Coronado and his followers. During stampedes caused by storms or the sight of herds of bison in the new land, many of their horses scattered and were lost to these and later Spanish adventurers. Perhaps some of the tired animals may have strayed away in search of water or feed. At any rate, there were thousands of them scattered over the plains. Bands roamed as far north as the head of the Loup River in Nebraska, but beyond that I have never found them, or heard old white trappers or Indians tell of having seen them.

When wagon roads cut across the plains to the farther West, horses and mules occasionally escaped and joined the bands of mustangs. Strangely, these gentler animals soon became even wilder and more watchful than the mustangs themselves. Certainly a few long-headed army mules I have seen among the roving bands were the most wisely wild creatures imaginable. Back in Missouri or some other state, or under the gentle care of some expert government muleskinner, they had acquired a knowledge of men and their ways, and their extremely delicate sense of smell enabled them to scent man at long range — especially a man announced by the expansive halo emerging from an old pipe or chawing plug.

A mule that had lived in the open with the mustangs for a time would become so watchful that the slightest scent of man, day or night, near or far, would cause it to snort with a wild terror that would stampede the entire band at topmost speed, and it would be many miles before they could muster enough control to look back to see what had caused the excitement.

A genuine danger against which the mustangs had to be on constant guard was the big wolf, or lobo. This cowardly pest was ever hungry for a taste of horseflesh. Weak or crippled horses and very young colts were easy prey, if the wolf could sneak up and slash their hamstrings with its sharp teeth before the defenders of the band discovered the enemy. But for a strong, active mare or stallion, a wolf might show some respect: a thoroughly enraged horse, fighting with its teeth, striking lightning-like blows with its forefeet, and playing a double tattoo with its heels, is no plaything for even a pack of wolves.

As the horses escaped from emigrant and freighting trains joined and mixed with them, purebred mustangs became more and more scarce. By 1880 they had almost disappeared from the plains. The few remaining today are to be found only among the herds of Indian ponies on some reservations where the policy of breeding up to get larger horses for farming or freighting has not been strictly followed. Now and then a pony having the conformation, coloring and marking of the mustang may be obtained from some one of the older Indians, who value the superb quality of this breed of horses too highly to allow them entirely to disappear.

Then there are the so-called "wild horses" to be found in a few places, but they are not true mustangs. They are range horses spoiled or gone wild, usually through someone's bad management or bad luck in trying to corral them. A sudden scare at the entrance to a corral, and the wild horses will turn and run for the range. One such attempt, if successful, makes them hard to corral again, and if they break back from the corral two or three times, they become a pretty badly spoiled lot. But these are not mustangs.

In the early seventies men were making a business of catching bands of mustangs and selling them in states east and north. There were three methods of catching wild horses. One way in which it was done was to trap them in corrals built in thickets back from the edge of the prairie. The chute leading to the corral narrowed at the entrance to the corral so that not more than three horses could enter abreast, thus preventing the trapped band from escaping before the heavy bar poles could be put up and lashed. V-shaped wings extended for a quarter of a mile or more out from the chute. Both wings and entrance were concealed by green brush.

When all was in readiness, a number of riders, widely separated and moving in a half-circle, would ride out of the timber and chaparral on the side of the prairie where the mustangs ranged. Of course, the horses would flee before the advancing cowboys. The riders at the two ends of the half-circle would make straight for the wings, while the rest, gradually getting closer together, kept the mustangs running always toward the corral. When the frightened band was well within the wings, its pursuers would close in, yelling and firing their pistols. The leaders of the excited horses, on the look-out for any opening in the green thicket concealing the wings, would rush through the opening at the narrow end of the chute, only to find themselves hopelessly trapped.

The fright of the horses can easily be imagined. Frantically, they would rush around and around the corral. Sometimes they would all make for one side, piling up so thickly that those farthest back were able to escape by climbing up and leaping from the piled-up mass of struggling horses. Many were crippled thus, and some died.

With the band once secured within the corral, the riders would depart and allow the terrorized animals to settle down for a few hours. When they returned, the real scare for the horses began, for the terrible looking creatures who had driven them into that pen now climbed down into it with them. Already exhausted from their previous efforts to escape, the mustangs soon became a panting, breathless mass of horseflesh. Old stallions that showed fight were promptly shot. Lassos were brought into play, and horses caught by the feet were thrown and secured with rawhide hobbles or clogs [1] placed on their front legs.

[1] Hobbles have long been in common use in the West, but so far as I know, clogs were used only in the brush country of southwestern Texas. They were strong forked sticks about an inch and a half in diameter, and about two feet in length, lashed with rawhide thongs to the front leg of a horse. Clogged, an animal could make little headway when it tried to run, and, as when hobbled, it soon tired of trying to go at speed.

When all the horses that had been neither maimed nor killed were secured, they were left in the corral until they became pretty hungry and thirsty. Then the bar poles were taken down, and the captives allowed to work their way out through the narrow chute into the wings, where there was usually a little waterhole or a creek. If they tried to get beyond the mouth of the wings the first day or so, there were the riders, to frighten them back.

Gradually they were given freedom to graze on the prairie during the daytime, and were driven back into the corral only at night. After a few days of this treatment, hobbles and clogs were removed from the horses which seemed most subdued. Within a few weeks the entire band would be freed of encumbrances, and could be driven in any direction desired.

I never took part in mustang hunts of this kind, but I did observe several. It was certainly a cruel performance.

A more humane way of capturing these fine animals was to walk them down. This method was followed successfully by a man with whom I hunted big game in Colorado and Wyoming, who later became known best as Wild Horse Charlie. He was, I think, the first man to make a large-scale business of catching mustangs on the open plains. Early in the spring of 1876 in eastern Colorado he captured several bands of wild horses, and drove them into Nebraska and Iowa to be sold.

Wild Horse Charlie's way of catching them was to make a camp on the range of the mustangs with two or three good riders, at a time when moonlight would aid in the work. It was well known to the plainsmen that mustangs had a habit of settling on a given range. From some good observation point a rider with field glasses would locate a band of horses. Early the morning after, the work of capturing them would begin.

A rider would approach the horses from the opposite direction to that in which he desired them to run. As mustangs have keen sight and are always on the lookout for danger, they would take to their heels the moment a rider came in view. This horseman would not race after them, but would follow fast enough to keep the band in sight. Other riders on watch would note the direction in which the mustangs started to circle, and in turn would take up the slow chase, while the man who had started it would go back to camp for a little rest, and to change his tired mount for a fresh one.

This relay system continued day and night, never allowing the mustangs to stop for either food or drink. For the first few days of the chase the wild horses would cover many miles of ground — a hundred miles in twenty-four hours was not unusual. On about the seventh or eighth day, or even sooner, the aged and weaker mustangs would play out and stop. Those that turned to put up a fight were shot. Other exhausted animals would be lassoed and hobbled or side-lined — a front and a hind foot on one side tied together. By about the tenth day all the mustangs were ready for capture, and would be brought under such control that they could be driven into some strong cattle corral.

Still another method, which was not used in capturing bands of mustangs, but only to get a particular horse considered especially valuable because of its beauty, color, marking, or speed, was "creasing." It is a method, however, that has been more talked about than successfully employed. To crease a horse one had first to get within close shooting distance of this most animated target. He must then place a rifle bullet in the top of its neck, grazing the cords just enough to stun the animal and knock it down so that it could be tied before it recovered from the shock. One had to be not only a mighty good shot, but extremely lucky, to make a success of this method. It was very easy to break the neck of the animal, or to give it a slight wound and a bad scare, or to score a clean miss.

I tried it once, but I never attempted to crease my second mustang. While gathering cattle I had several times caught sight of a band led by one of the handsomest stallions I had ever seen. He was cream color, with heavy mane and tail. His mane was parted equally, and hung neatly down both sides of his neck. A black stripe ran down his back and around one of his legs.

This little band, I discovered, had the habit of drinking from a pool located in the washout of a creek bed which could be approached only from one side, the other three sides of the washout having high vertical banks. These creek banks leading to the waterhole made wings that were about a hundred and fifty feet long. I figured that if I could hide near this watering place until all the horses coming to drink were within the runway, I could dash into the mouth of it, and as the mustangs rushed past me to escape, I could crease the handsome stallion with my six-shooter. (At that time I considered myself hard to beat, either mounted or on foot, with my pistol.)

After weeks of waiting, my opportunity came. While hunting one day for some saddle horses that had strayed from camp, I sighted the band trailing toward the waterhole. Keeping out of sight, I beat them to the place and concealed myself and my horse in dense chaparral about a hundred yards from the mouth of the runway. The horses seemed not to sense the danger, for they rushed in a bunch to the water, where they made such a noise splashing and pawing about that they did not hear me approaching.

When I rode into the runway, however, they certainly got up some action. As the stallion came dashing madly by, I fired. Down he went, and I rushed to him.

But when I went to tie him, I found I had broken his neck. I could have cried; probably I did. I know that I felt remorseful to have taken the life of that beautiful creature. If only I had used my lasso instead of my six-shooter, he would either have escaped or been mine.

Another time, while out after our saddle horses, I found among them a young mustang stallion. Evidently he had been run out of his band by older stallions, for he was badly bitten up. As I came upon him he was standing with his head down, fast asleep. Even when I rode within twenty feet of him, he did not move. Seeing my chance, I took my rope quietly from the horn of the saddle, and threw a loop over his head.

When the rope touched him, he surely woke up and tried to leave me. But no, his wild-horse days were over. I had to choke him down before I could get a war bridle of rope over his proud head. In a short time I had broken him to lead. I took him to camp, trained him to a picket rope, and broke him to the saddle. He grew to be a great pet, and proved to be one of the best horses I ever owned.

Then I invented a way of my own to capture wild horses, but I wouldn't recommend it to others. A year or so later I noticed on the trail a band of saddle horses which had gone wild. Nearly every day this band would stand for a time under the shade of a solitary mesquite tree on a little bit of prairie. They were all fat and sleek, and I thought it would be fine to catch one, and give my saddle horse a rest.

One morning I took my rope and walked out to the lone tree, only about a mile from our cow camp. After making a loop at one end of the lasso, and tying the other end to a strong limb, I climbed into the tree to wait, holding the loop in my hand.

For hours I stayed there on my perch. Just as I was beginning to feel a bit foolish about my position, and had about given up hope of snaring a horse, I sighted the band, headed my way. With great deliberation they walked over every other spot on the prairie for what seemed to me about ten times, before they ambled over to the shade of the tree where I was waiting. I had not dared to move all this while, for fear of frightening them; I was so badly cramped when they did come that I could hardly move. They seemed to have not the slightest idea that danger lurked above.

When they were directly under me, I looked the band over carefully, and picked out the horse I considered the best of the bunch. Then, tipping the loop slightly, I let it drop. It went right over the head of the chosen horse, and I chuckled to see him jump when it struck him. He leaped with a snort, and went away fast. I didn't laugh long, for when he had traveled the length of the rope, he didn't stop, and the rope didn't break; the limb to which it was fastened did, however, and *I* was sitting on that limb. Down I went like a rock.

It was my turn to be astonished. I had not

given that part of my trick any thought. It was a bad bump, and the only comfort I had was that no one witnessed it. I was up in a moment, following the trail of the horse and the heavy limb he was hauling. He wasn't hard to locate. He dashed into the nearby timber, and soon had himself so wound up that I could walk right up to him. After working a few minutes I put a noose over his nose and lower jaw, and led him to camp. When I arrived I asked one of the Mexicans to get on him, for I had had enough fun for one day. He bucked a little, but soon gave up, and came to be a good cow horse. I rode him until we left that country, and then turned him loose to run wild again.

XVII : CAPORAL MAC

Early in March of 1875 another herd was ready at the Slaughter ranch to be taken northward, and I was ready to go with it. Our caporal for this year's drive was to be McNeil — Mac — Stewart, regarded by big cattle owners as one of the best in the business. I found him to be a genial man, and a leader who knew how to handle not only cattle, but his cow waddies as well.

Mac differed in many respects from other caporales. In his early boyhood he had been exposed to schooling that "took." He was a good penman, and no cattleman could find fault with his spelling or with his dealing with figures. He and his friend Dick Head both took a kindly interest in me. Mac felt that I was able to handle the downstream point of the herd — the critical point when crossing rivers on our way north. I was very proud of this confidence.

During the struggle between the northern and the southern states, Mac had been in the cavalry of the Confederate forces. One of the experiences he related made a lasting impression on me.

He and a few other soldiers, known to be good rifle shots, had been detailed by the commanding officer to scatter along the banks of the Red River to pick off the pilots of transports that were taking supplies to northern troops. This was a duty that required each man to work alone. A place for concealment had to be located, at a point on the river where the channel came close enough to the bank to give the hidden sharpshooter a close range on the pilots.

Officers on the transports, fully apprehending the danger, would shell with grape and canister any place where they suspected enemy riflemen might be lurking.

On his first attempt to carry out orders, Mac found a hiding place that looked favorable, sighted a boat coming upstream, and waited. Officers aboard, perhaps sensing danger, sent a boat ashore with a detachment of picked men, with orders to kill or capture any Confederate sharpshooter they might find. The Federal scouts advanced slowly, taking advantage of cover afforded by trees and brush, and scanning the river bank. Mac was hardly expecting this attack from the rear, and made some move that was seen by the enemy. His rifle was lying near, ready for action, but when a voice called on him to surrender, and a glance over his shoulder revealed several rifles pointed at him, he obeyed promptly.

Soon he found himself aboard the transport, in heavy irons, and set up as a target for the rifles of his Confederate allies. His captors tied him in the wheelhouse in a position to afford protection to the pilot from other sharpshooters along the banks. Mac's friends stationed farther upstream did their best to shoot that wheelhouse and its helmsman to bits, but luckily neither the prisoner nor the pilot was hit, although Mac declared that splinters of wood, and hot lead, were plentiful all about him to the end of the trip. By some good fortune (which he did not reveal), he escaped not long after his capture.

Mac was a small man, weighing about one hundred and forty pounds. His body was well built, and he had fine features. His manners were those of a gentleman. I never heard him ask whether a horse would pitch; he would simply vault into the saddle at the proper moment, and though he often got a bucker, I never saw him thrown. He did not use spurs, and he seldom hit a horse with a quirt. I never saw him carry a six-shooter in his belt, or a rifle on his saddle. He kept a rifle in the mess wagon, when trailing herds. Having seen him shoot on several occasions, I knew how well he could. He never used profane language or tried to look the part of a dangerous man.

Mac's spirits, when all hands were put to the test by bad weather or stampedes or some other fortune of the trail, revealed his steady humor. He would ride up to me when I was so tired and uncomfortable that I could hardly keep the saddle, and with one of his smiles would remark, "I surely wouldn't like to be a cow waddie, but it's fun to be a caporal." Knowing well that he was getting the same full measure of hardship his men had to endure, besides assuming responsibility for all losses of cattle, I could only try to look pleased with my lot, and show him that I was still on deck.

Sometimes Mac would ride up to an object lying on the ground not far from the herd, and examine it. I would ride to the object after he had left it, and generally I would find something written on it, such as, "This is the skull of Mac Stewart when he was a buffalo"; or "Jim Cook's skull when he was a lobo." He knew perfectly well that I would try to see what he had written on his find.

The only time I ever saw him lose his temper was when we were trying to get our mess wagon and provisions across the Red River on a raft we had made. We had no trouble with Indians on that trip, but it rained and poured, and then rained some more, from the very start until we reached the Kansas line. We had to swim most of the streams, and often make a raft out of the wagon box or anything else we could float, in order to get our supplies across.

Mac was on top of the cargo, trying to keep goods from being lost. He had taken off his boots and thrown them on top of the load. Just as the raft neared the north bank of the river, where

I sat on my horse, one of his boots rolled off into the rushing water. I saw Mac snatch the other boot and hurl it furiously after the one that had gone overboard. I laughed, but it seemed less funny shortly, when I discovered that my own boots, which had been on the raft, were also washed away.

Mac and I were in a pretty pickle, sure enough. The nearest place where we could buy boots was in the Indian Territory, at Camp Supply. That afternoon I discovered an Indian camp a mile or so off our trail, where I bought two pairs of moccasins.

Moccasins might do for Indians, but for a cowboy they protected the wrong places and exposed the sensitive ones. Our insteps and ankles being vulnerable, and our stirrups old-fashioned wooden ones, we badly bruised our feet and ankles. The buckskin would get water-soaked, and wet buffalo chips made a poor fire to dry them, after a hard day's work.

Once when the caporal and I sat trying to get some of the water out of our soggy footgear, he suggested that we swap, just for a day, to see if it would bring better weather. As our legs and feet were bleeding, I told Mac that the blood on my moccasins might poison him, but he said that if we swapped, we would soon be blood kin. This is typical of the spirit with which he met obstacles.

Where the country wasn't afloat, it was a mass of mud, almost bad enough to bog down a jacksnipe.

The caporal and I continued to have foot trouble a-plenty until we reached Camp Supply, and bought other foot covers which served until we could get real cowhand boots to replace those that had gone down the river.

During that extremely wet spell, when moccasins were not in style but were endured by a caporal and his cow waddie, not only the men but the horses and cattle became fagged out. The herd was a large one, made up of all ages of cattle except calves. The longhorns were decidedly inclined, night and day, to stampede. In the deep mud all about us we could, after the first couple of days had tired the cattle, force the herd to mill before they ran far. But what an unpleasant mess it was! When we got them going in a circle, the ground over which they tramped would be churned into a "loblolly," a foot or more deep. As they became exhausted from milling, we would shake our coats at them and encourage them by yelling to keep turning the mill. This was intended to cure them of the habit of stampeding.

Before clear days came we had an experience with a tornado which I wouldn't care to repeat. Arriving at the Canadian River in Indian Territory, we had camped on the south side of the stream, waiting for it to subside a bit before attempting to cross. About noon it became evident that we were in for a severe storm. Never had I seen such queer-looking clouds. They seemed all to be rushing toward the center of the heavens, and we could hear a steady, sullen roar which seemed to come from all directions. Hastily, we staked the wagon to the ground and lashed down its canvas cover with extra ropes.

I was on herd with the horses. Everybody but the cook and me went with the cattle. Our band of horses I kept close to the wagon. We were as nearly ready as we could make ourselves for the oncoming storm when hailstones began to strike all about us. In a few moments we were struck by a truly awful blast of wind, hailstones, and water. The horses that were not hobbled, stampeded; I raced ahead of them, trying to check them. So thick was the air with hail and water that I could not see ten feet. The stones were hammering my head so fiercely that it seemed to be on fire. I would put one arm over my head until it was pelted as much as it could stand, then would shift to the other.

Suddenly I came to a gulch fifteen feet deep, with banks not quite vertical, but steep enough. I could neither turn my horse nor stop him. Over we went, with one hundred badly frightened horses at our heels. My horse landed on his feet, but slipped and fell in the middle of the gulch. The rest of the animals came over, tumbling all about me. I managed to hold my horse until the herd had passed, and then suddenly I could hold him no longer; he jerked away and off through the storm.

By this time water was pouring in a torrent

down the little gulch where I lay. I had to get out of the way quickly or be drowned, for the water soon rose to seven or eight feet. I crawled to the top of the bank and drifted with the storm, the hailstones raising blood blisters on my face and hands. I traveled about a quarter of a mile, and came to a comparatively level country. Even there, I was in water and ice nearly to my knees. My head and face and hands were one solid bruise. I was utterly played out. I was sure my time had come; I was sure the rest of the boys were dead. The roar of the storm was terrifying. Any minute I knew I could expect some huge hailstone to knock me senseless; if it did, I would drown in the icy lake at my feet. All I could do was to stand and wait for my destiny, praying one minute for the Lord to save me, and wondering the next if my body would ever be found.

As suddenly as it had come, the storm passed, and there I stood in two feet of ice water, with no land in sight in any direction. Shaking with cold, and hardly able to keep my feet, I began to walk (or rather, wade), to try to warm myself. The water went down rapidly, and soon I found places where I could get out of it. A mile or more away was a high hill, and I struck out for it, hoping to see something familiar from its top. I had no idea where camp was.

Reaching the crest of the hill, I sighted the timber along the Canadian River, and knew about where the wagon should be. Not a hoof of cattle or horses could be seen in any direction. I walked slowly toward the river, wondering if everybody had been killed, and what I should do. Then, coming up over another hill, I saw an object lying on the prairie half a mile off. At first it was unrecognizable, but finally I made out that it was a man. I was surely glad to see him; he was one of our boys.

He had been with the cattle when the storm burst, and was riding an outlaw horse, to give his better mounts a rest. He knew that the fractious animal would start pitching in a hail storm, and prevent his helping to hold the herd; so the minute the hailstones began to strike, he dismounted and unsaddled the horse. To give himself some protection from the pounding hail, he put his saddle and saddle blanket over his shoulders and squatted on the prairie to wait for better weather. His horse jerked loose and ran away.

The cowboy had chosen a valley, rather a poor refuge, to wait the storm out. Hardly had he fixed himself under his saddle shelter when several feet of water flooded him out. He backed up the hill, with his saddle over his head. This was not very satisfactory shelter, but even so, he was not as badly hammered by the hail as I was.

We went on to camp together, and found the cook safe, but full of his own experiences. Though the wagon had been staked down and secured with ropes, it had been upset, and the ropes torn loose. The cook was kept busy trying to find shelter from the punishing hail and flying skillets and coffee pots. But he had fared better than the rest of the crew, for the wagon was out of the center of the storm.

We went down to the timber, dragged some wood to camp, and soon had a pot of heartening coffee boiling, and our clothes drying. After a little, one of the boys from the cattle herd came back to camp and reported the herd and the boys safe. The longhorns had stampeded and run for several miles, passing through a big camp of Cheyenne Indians, and adding, no doubt, to the terror of *their* situation. As the storm had circled, the cattle had at last run out of it, and the stampede was stopped. A cowboy had been sent in to see what had become of the wagon and horses.

By this time I was ready to report for duty. I took the cowboy's horse and rode to a hill to sight our missing horse herd, if I could. Off in a direction nearly opposite to that taken by the herd when it left me in the gulch, I saw some animals. I was sure they were not ours, but I thought I might be able to drive them to camp, and thus have mounts to use in hunting our strays. To my surprise and relief, I found that they were our horses. The storm had driven them almost in a circle.

I had found out what a tornado could do, and how it felt to be caught on the edge of one. In the center of its path, not more than a quarter of a mile from our wagon, it had torn out great trees growing along the river, and piled them in tangled, twisted masses, carrying some of them hundreds of feet. Little willows growing on the river bottom were still rooted, but their bark was twisted and stripped from them. Had the center of the tornado struck our outfit, there would have been some badly scrambled horses, cattle, and cowboys, with a small amount of trail cook and mess wagon thrown in, lying all about the Indian Territory.

The strip of country covered by the destructive center of this tornado was about half a mile wide. Hail lay in drifts three feet deep in the low places. Thousands of prairie dogs and little prairie-dog owls, rabbits, rattlesnakes, and other small wild creatures, had been drowned out of their holes and been frozen or beaten to death by the hail. Even the grass was smashed off at the roots and washed away with drifts of hailstones. Luck surely was with us that day.

Finally we reached Kansas and its lively cow towns. Branch trails led to Newton, Abilene, Ellsworth, and Great Bend, busy centers during the cattle-trail months. Quite a large part of their populations during the busy season was made up of gamblers and tough women. Buffalo hunters and freighters, emigrants and soldiers, and an occasional bunch of trail-weary cowboys, added to the general liveliness. All except clergymen packed a gun or two, or kept them within mighty close reach. Any dispute had to be settled with guns or knives. "A man or two for breakfast" was not considered sufficiently unusual to cause comment. Dance halls and gambling places were the breeding grounds of the troubles that sometimes led to manslaughter, aided by the fire-water sold over the many bars.

When the cattle we had brought up the trail had been sold, I returned with our men to Texas, to the work of gathering longhorns. Mac Stewart continued trailing herds up from Texas. Among the men he worked for was one who engaged him to go to Mexico to take charge of mining property he owned there. The other foreman, Mac was told, was misusing funds from the property, and having a fine time with the money, posing as a prince of good fellows among the sporting element of the city of Parral.

From letters I received later from Stewart, I learned the rest of the story. When he reached Parral to assume his new duties, Mac went to the office and told the manager he was to take over. Incensed, the manager went out and told his friends he was being ousted. He returned to the office with reinforcements, opened the door, and took a shot at Stewart, slightly wounding him. Mac was unarmed, but seizing a Winchester that stood in the corner of the room, he shot his assailant, killing him outright. When he stepped to the door, he saw that the friends the manager had brought were police. They began firing, and Mac killed the nearest man with his last cartridge.

Then, dropping the gun, he surrendered, and was thrown into jail.

The situation was critical. For an American to kill a policeman in Mexico, no matter what the provocation, was a deadly offense. In addition, Mac was one of the hated Tejanos, against whom the Mexicans held a violent antagonism. Still fresh in their minds was the bloody war over the territory of Texas. No Texan could, therefore, hope for leniency when in their hands.

For a long time Mac was held without a hearing, and finally he was sent to a Mexican prison. The next ten years must have been a nightmare to him. Confined in damp, bare cells; given just enough food to keep body and soul together; and forced to undergo further unendurable hardships, he clung to life under conditions that wore down his resistance and reduced him to a skeleton.

During this time I received many letters from him, evidently smuggled through by a guard, describing the horrors of his situation, and begging his friends to intercede for him while he still had life. But the efforts of his friends in Texas and over the range country of the West were futile. Porfirio Diaz, then President of Mexico, was firm: there were certain rules for foreigners who broke the laws of Mexico; these had to be obeyed.

At last Mac was taken to the prison at Chihuahua. When being transferred from one prison to another, he was often prodded with bayonets by his guards, and made to ride bareback on a mule, to which he was fastened with irons. It was but a continuation in spirit of the treatment accorded prisoners of war during our war with Mexico. At Chihuahua his treatment was little better, although some of the money and food and clothing sent him by his friends reached and comforted him. I sent him some packages. But this prison, like the rest, was dirty, infested with vermin, poorly ventilated.

Mac's many friends in the States kept up their efforts in his behalf, and at last, through the intercession of the State Legislature of Texas, his freedom was granted. He came back to Texas emaciated, and broken in health. When, escorted by a Mexican guard, Mac Stewart was received at the boundary line at El Paso by a group of friends and legislators, there was a reunion of heartbreaking sadness. His terrible experiences had so weakened him that he did not linger long to enjoy his return to friends and freedom.

I remember Mac Stewart as a kindly, courageous, and efficient caporal. He was a man without fear, and with a sense of humor that carried him through hardships in a way to inspire his men. He was a true and valued friend.

XVIII : TRAIL ADVENTURES

I left the Slaughter outfit soon after the trail drive with Mac Stewart, to work for a cattleman named Bishop, who came with his partner, Mr. Halff, to the Slaughter ranch to buy cattle to stock their pastures. They needed help, and Ben Slaughter recommended me.

My new work was different from brush popping. Bishop and Halff's business was the buying of bunches of cattle from ranchmen, and then throwing the longhorns into big pastures preparatory to having them driven northward. I helped to receive and brand these cattle, and to trail them to the pastures.

One of the first bunches we got was a spoiled herd. For stampeding, they were the worst animals I ever dealt with. The very first night, after we had them branded and were starting to drive them out of the brush, they stampeded. When daylight came I was about the only man still with them, for the other cowboys, and even the foreman, Burton, had never chased wild cattle through the mesquite, cactus, and chaparral, and they were afraid to let their horses run.

Next day I persuaded Burton to hire some Mexicans who were used to brush running, but in spite of the good help these vaqueros gave us, we lost about six hundred head before we reached the nearest big corral. There Mr. Bishop joined us, and asked Burton and me to go back into the brush and recapture some of the lost cattle, if we could. He promised that if we did, he would give me charge of a pasture.

We hired some Mexicans to help, and headed back into the Texas jungle; and for three weeks we had a picnic in the brush. Fortunately, while branding the cattle, we had bobbed off their tails, and this made it easy to distinguish our animals from others. A number of them were brought in during the first week. By then all the others were mixed with the wild cattle, and each one that was caught had to be roped. We got back most of that lost herd, but we nearly wore out the horses in doing it.

When we had all that were worth bothering about, we trailed them back to the main herd. Mr. Bishop was pleased, and as he had promised, he put me in charge of a big pasture, with two men to assist me in taking care of the cattle. Our main job was to make sure the fences were secure, and to see that the herd was kept within them.

However, before letting me take up my new

duties as a pasture boss, Mr. Bishop took me along with him as guard on a trip to purchase cattle. In those days paper currency and bank checks were not in use, and gold coin was the base of all business transactions. We carried gold in canvas sacks on a pack mule, paying it out as Mr. Bishop bought bunches of cattle. We realized the danger of carrying gold coin, but it was necessary in order to do business. At night, when Mr. Bishop and I occupied the same bedding-roll, I slept with one eye open, but my companion, having been a pioneer and stage driver on the San Antonio-Austin road, took things calmly, and slept.

Mr. Bishop was looking for horses as well as cattle on this purchasing trip. I was given much of the responsibility of choosing and trying out the saddle animals. In San Antonio there was a corral, later called a livery barn, where horses whose owners failed to pay their feed bills could often be bought at bargain prices. There I found a horse which pleased me very much. He was a perfect little animal, powerfully muscled, short coupled, round bodied, and deep through the chest. He had large eyes and a small head, and he was mouse color, with a broad black stripe the entire length of his back and about his forelegs. He had all the color markings of the mustangs. This horse had reverted to its forebears, not only in marking, but in the high arched neck and beautiful body. I found I could have him for eight dollars, and I paid it quickly.

This beautiful little animal I selected as a mount for myself not only for the remainder of that trip, but later on the trail. I called him Tejon, meaning gray. He soon learned several tricks from me, such as kneeling when I saddled him, and lying down so that I could shoot over him. He was surefooted and traveled high in front, never stumbling, and having what we would call in these days "good knee action." I used Tejon exclusively as my night horse, and was very fond of him.

About the middle of February Mr. Bishop told me that MacNiel Stewart was to take one of his herds north that season, and that I might go with him if I wanted to. I was glad to be with my old caporal. Mac came a little later and took me to the Indian Bend pasture on the Nueces, where we gathered a herd and rolled out. Shortly we added two hundred of the spoiled cattle which had given Burton and me such trouble, and they spoiled all the others. The devils would stampede several times in a night, and they kept this up all the way.

By the time we reached the Indian Territory we were nearly played out. It had rained a great deal, and we had lost much sleep. Once, when we had been up all night in a storm and had ridden hard all the next day in the downpour, at night every old cow man in the outfit quit the herd, went to camp, and lay down in the mud. They said they couldn't stand any more.

Only the younger cowboys, that is, those under thirty, stayed with the herd during this tough spell. Mac was with the cattle all the time. He would have died in his saddle rather than let them escape him. I was nearly dead myself, and had to revive my old trick of putting tobacco juice on my eyelids to keep awake. By this time the cattle were so worn out that they couldn't run, but they kept drifting about all night.

When morning broke the sun came out warm and bright, and the herd, after grazing a while, lay down to rest, giving us a chance to catch up on our eating. We had gone hungry while there were only soaked buffalo chips with which to try to make a fire. One of the men who had been in camp all night came to watch the herd while the rest of us got four or five hours' sleep. Mac said nothing to the deserters, but it was plain that they would never again go on the trail with him.

Every creek and river was at flood stage. The Brazos, when we reached it, was surely on a rampage. We had crossed so many streams that we had little trouble getting the longhorns started into the torrent. Our lead cattle, with me as right point driver on a swimming horse crowding them against the rapid current, were well into the river, when suddenly a big tree rose out of the water in front and frightened them. They began swimming around in twenty feet of water. I tried my best to break up the milling, but more tree tops kept rising out of the river to plague us all.

The point driver on the upstream side, Ad Spaugh, arriving at the edge of the water, saw that I was in trouble. He could not swim, but he made his horse jump off a high bank into the water, and attempted to come to my rescue. His horse would not swim, so the cowboy slipped off and sought to grab his tail, in order to keep his own head above water. It ended by my having to rescue him. By the time I got to him, I could see only one of his hands. I grabbed it, and towed him ashore, where he soon recovered from his overdose of Brazos water, and at the present time is living as a rancher in Wyoming, not far from my home in Nebraska.

We had seen a good many buffalo on our way north, and I killed several that came near the herd. The great herds were rapidly being exterminated by hide hunters. At Fort Griffin I saw near the sutler's store a pile of buffalo hides at least fifty yards square and ten feet high. Wholesale slaughter was rapidly clearing the plains of those fine game animals.

Just before we reached the Cimarron River, Caporal Mac, who had been riding a mile or two ahead of the herd, came back. "Jim," he said, "there are five or six buffalo coming straight for the herd. If you want some fun, catch your best horse and go for them. Get some good fat meat."

A few days before, I had overheard one of the boys in camp say that shooting a buffalo in the head would not kill it. He insisted that no bullet would go through its thick hair and skull. I had declared that the first chance I got, I would kill a buffalo by shooting it in the forehead. The boys laughed at me, but I told them to wait a few days before they laughed too hard. Here was my chance to show them.

A part of this story is the fact that I had had to buy at Fort Griffin a pair of pants many sizes too large, since they had no boys' sizes. I had cut off the legs to make the overalls short enough, and I tucked the legs into my boot tops. The waist I could only wrap about me, buckling my cartridge belt good and tight to hold up the overalls.

I rode out to the horse herd and caught Roper. Now Roper was as good a cow horse as ever breathed, but when it came to buffalo hunting, he did not know it all. I jumped on him bareback, taking my Winchester carbine, but leaving my cartridge belt and revolver behind. I wanted to ride light, for it was a very sandy country.

All at once the buffalo came in sight, and I headed for them, keeping out of view until I was close. Then I dashed out into the open. First I overtook a two-year-old bull, and in passing shot at him and saw him fall. Riding on swiftly, I was soon close enough to a fine large bull to give him what was called a kidney shot. Down he went, as if with a broken back. I left him standing on his forelegs, with his hind quarters dragging, and I started for camp to get some of the boys to come out and see me finish the big animal.

On the way I had to pass the spot where I had shot the younger bull, and to my astonishment he had disappeared. Riding to the top of a little hill near by and looking around, I saw him heading full speed for our wagon. The cook had stopped to get dinner near a lone tree which somehow had managed to survive the hardships of that barren country. He had stretched a rope from the wagon wheel to the tree, and had it covered with meat he was jerking.

Three or four men were in camp, and there were several rifles in the wagon when that buffalo was sighted. But neither cook nor cowboys thought to grab a gun and shoot the charging animal. One man went up the tree, and the rest dived into the wagon. Looking neither right nor left, that bull kept on a bee line for Alaska. He struck the rope about halfway between tree and wagon. Somebody remembered to reach for a rifle when the bull was about a quarter of a mile by the wagon. It was now my turn to laugh.

"Why didn't you shoot?" I asked as I rode into camp.

They looked around sheepishly at each other, as if to say, "Why didn't we, I wonder?"

"Now, then," I continued, "if some of you brave fellows will go with me, I will show you whether a buffalo can be killed by shooting it in the head. I don't need a rifle; I'll kill him with my pistol."

I left my rifle in camp, and stuck the loaded

pistol in my boot top. Some of the men rode out with me to the wounded bull. When we came in sight, he began to flounder and shake his shaggy head. Our cow ponies would not go near him, so I said, "If one of you fellows will hold my horse, I'll walk up and shoot him."

Handing my reins to one of the boys, I jumped down, pistol in one hand, the other holding up my overalls, and advanced towards the bull. He was about as furious with pain and rage as a buffalo can be, and I did not shoot immediately because he was tossing his head, making it impossible to hit him squarely in the forehead. I got within ten feet, and stopped. As I stood there aiming the revolver and waiting for the opportune moment to nail him, he made a supreme effort, rose on all four feet, and made a furious lunge at me!

All thought of shooting suddenly left me. I whirled and started to run, forgetting all about my loose overalls, which instantly dropped down around my feet and completely hobbled me. Over I went on my face. I turned over to meet my death face to face, and found that the buffalo was down for good. His back had not been quite broken by my bullet, but his wild plunge for me had finished the work. His head was within six feet of me. I jumped up quickly, walked closer, and sent a bullet through his brain.

I walked back to my horse, and casually asked the boys what they thought of my style of killing a buffalo. Some of them were as pale as I was.

"Your luck beats all science," someone said.

On the way back to camp, I showed the boys where I had knocked down the little bull. Probably I had just creased him, and when he got on his feet again he was more or less crazy and just ran in the direction in which he happened to be headed. The boys said he never looked at the wagon as he passed, and that his eyes were bright red.

At camp the whole story was retold, accompanied by remarks such as, "Next time Mac sends you buffalo hunting, Jim, you'd better take somebody along to hold up your pants."

Another crazy animal gave me a narrow escape at the end of this drive. We had taken the cattle to Dodge City, Kansas, and from there to Ogalalla, Nebraska. They had been sold to Major Frank North and William F. Cody (Buffalo Bill), who were establishing a ranch near the head of Dismal River.

I was helping Dick Head cut some cattle from the herd, while Major North sat on his horse near us. The horse I was riding was hard to beat at cutting out cattle, but he had the bad habit of taking the bit, throwing his nose high, and bolting with his rider. At such times he would not look where he was headed, but with eyes fixed toward the sky, would plunge over anything in his path.

The horse chose this particular time to put on a show, and headed for the Major. Trying to hold him in always made him throw his head higher and run harder, so I just gave him his way. The only method I had found that stopped him was to quirt and spur him for a quarter of a mile or more, when he would be so winded that I could circle him around and get him back to work.

When the horse started to run, I shouted to the Major to get out of the way, but evidently he thought I was fooling and could rein in the runaway, and he made no move to clear the track. As a result we struck his horse amidships and knocked him flat, on top of the rider. Then my horse fell, threw me on my head, and rolled partly over me. Some of the boys helped me to the river bank and poured water over me. When I could recall what had happened, I asked for my horse, for I wanted to go at once and kill that "idiotic granger" who had let me run into him when he had plenty of time to get out of the way.

Major North had been hurt, but not so badly as I. His horse rose at once, and the Major rode to Dick Head, saying he "would like to kill that idiotic cow-puncher." He insisted that I had made no attempt to stop my horse, but had ridden straight at him and tried to run him down.

Dick had a good laugh, and then explained that taken alone, I was quite harmless, but that that horse and I together made a terrific combination. Then Dick rode over to see how I was getting on. I told him that my business just then was to remove that granger for letting me run into him. Dick explained who the granger was, and I permitted myself to be led over and introduced. Mutual explanations and apologies followed.

It was on this trip that I too saw some unusual things in the sky: the first really great mirage I had ever seen. Riding one day on the right-hand point of the herd, which we had strung out for two miles, I saw the lead cattle stop and begin to bunch up. To get them moving again I rode ahead. My first thought was that a coiled rattlesnake on the trail might have stopped the leaders, but when I approached cautiously, I saw that they were gazing, not at the ground ahead, but at something high above their heads.

Looking up into the sky toward where the eyes of the longhorns seemed to be focused, I was amazed to see what seemed to be a giant mule. The long-eared apparition appeared to be a hundred feet or more above us. Its legs were spread far apart, and its great ears were drooping. To quiet the cattle, I rode toward this monstrosity, and as I approached it, the gigantic apparition grew smaller and smaller, until I arrived within twenty-five feet of the awful object, and saw only a baby donkey, not more than an hour or two old. Probably it had been born while its mother was being driven with a herd of donkeys to miners in Colorado. The little creature could not walk, but could stand by bracing itself with its legs wide apart.

All animals born on the trail were usually shot at once, since they could not be cared for and it was unthinkable to leave them to perish. For some reason this baby had been overlooked. I quickly ended its life and dragged it with my lasso out of sight of the cattle. Then I rode quietly back to the leaders, and soon had the herd strung out once more and headed for the North Pole. A rider working with lead cattle was trained never to allow himself or his horse to show any sign of nervousness, for it would spread quickly to the wild, temperamental cattle that were the ones always to take the lead in trail drives.

Another time I saw a similar mirage while trailing a herd through the western part of the territory near Camp Supply. We were following a wagon road at the time, and this time, too, I was on the right point of the herd, when I saw coming toward me, high up in the air, a team and buggy. It was of a size such as I had never seen before. At that time I had had no experience with these dilating mirages, and felt uncertain as I rode ahead to investigate. I found some men driving an ordinary team and buggy, which gradually came down to earth and assumed normal size as I rode toward them. They were two Texas cattlemen driving from Dodge City south to meet their herds on the northward trail. Before they could frighten the cattle, I begged them to drive around a little distance, instead of in the line they were following, and they were decent enough to oblige me.

XIX : SIOUX PARLEY

In 1876, the year of Custer's tragic defeat by the Sioux, I helped drive a herd of about twenty-five hundred Texas steers from the Nueces River to the Whetstone Bottom on the Missouri River, Dakota. These cattle were owned by men who had contracted with the United States Department of the Interior to supply some of the Indian agencies with beef. The herd, being strong cattle, made good time and led the drive that season. It was the first great herd to be driven through western Nebraska into Dakota.

Our experiences in getting as far as the North Platte River were not unusual to those who drove the trail in those days — high water, stormy weather, stampedes, hunger at times, great thirst, and other discomforts designed to harrass the cowboy.

We crossed the South and North Platte rivers a few miles east of the town of Ogalalla. Thence we drove to Birchwood Creek, and on to the headwaters of the Dismal and Loup rivers, and north through the great chain of shifting sandhills, now so well known. There were ten men in the outfit, including Mac Stewart and the cook. In addition to our regular crew we had a guide, Aaron Barker, who had been taken on at North Platte City. Barker knew western Nebraska as well as any man living, probably, having dealt with the Sioux in that part of the country for years. He and some others had been employed in handling many Sioux ponies at the expense of their rightful owners, or so I was told.

We passed through the sandhill country at the season when the sand cherries were ripe and at their best, as were the blossoms of the soapweeds. The cattle seemed to find here something that pleased their palates, so that men and cattle were soon so scattered over the grazing ground that at one time it looked to me as if we should never get together again.

Driving on northward from the headwaters of the north fork of the Loup River, our guide led us toward one of the sandhill lakes. It was a long drive, without water, until we reached the lake, and the weather was very hot. When the cattle scented the water, long before we came in sight of it, they strung out and headed for it at a trot. We tried to hold the leaders back, but when we were within half a mile of the lake the herd split into bunches, and in spite of us, they rushed madly for the water and plunged in. About a hundred head became mired down — among them, some of our best cattle — before we could crowd the others to a spot in the lake where the mud and guano were less deep.

Before we could expect to eat supper, we had to save the cattle. This proved to be a hard task, for our horses would also get mired, trying to get in close enough to the cattle to enable us to rope them and pull them out. Fortunately there was a clump of willows at one side of the lake, and from these we cut and tied great bunches to use as a road, over which our horses or work oxen could pass without becoming mired. Every longhorn we got out of the mud was ready and willing to fight all mankind, the moment it got on its feet after being dragged to solid ground. One horse was badly gored by taking chances.

When the herd had made its uproarious descent upon the lake it had startled flocks of ducks, geese, pelicans, swans, and other varieties of wild water fowl, which now hovered over us and flew about us, astonished at our intrusion, probably. And when that night, in the small hours, something frightened the cattle, these wild neighbors must have wondered greatly at the sounds of thundering hoofs and clashing horns, and the other lesser noises made by herders yelling as they crowded and swung the point of the stampede back into the rapidly following mass of cattle, or singing the old Texas Lullaby when they gained control over the herd at last. We soon left them to their lonely paradise, however, for we recovered practically all the mired cattle, and continued along the trail.

When we had started north of the Platte rivers, all of us knew that we were entering a country, much of which was regarded by the Sioux as belonging by inheritance, and also by treaty rights, to their people. Many of the Sioux and Cheyenne bands were strongly opposed to the invasion of the Black Hills country by the white gold-seekers. A bridge just being completed across the North Platte was making accessible to thousands of fortune hunters lands where they expected to enrich themselves, with little labor or expense, simply by picking up gold.

Most of our outfit had had experience in trailing herds through country infested with Indians who had all sorts of questions regarding the right of the white man to travel through or make trails across their hunting grounds. The dangers risked regularly by those who opened up the cattle trails made them somewhat careless of the possibility of being wiped out by Indians. Everyone went armed with a heavy revolver and a knife; only a few carried rifles. The added weight of a gun on one side of a horse caused saddle galls which had to be strictly guarded against on eighteen-hundred-mile drives, for often life as well as the successful completion of such a drive hinged upon the condition of the horses.

On this trip it happened that I was the only

man who owned a rifle. This was carried in the wagon when I was not using it to shoot a little game for a change of diet. There were many elk, deer, and antelope about. We had seen few Indians, and none came near us on our outward drive with the cattle; but on our return trip to the Platte we found some — or rather, they found us.

We left the guide and wagon when the cattle were delivered to the contractors, and used pack ponies for the return trip. One day about noon, we camped for dinner on the northern bank of the Niobrara River, which at that point and at that season of the year was about fifty yards wide and four feet deep, with a swift current and much quicksand. Just as our coffee and bacon were ready, we saw an Indian ride into full view on the bluffs which skirted the river valley lands, about half a mile away. He signaled with both horse and blanket, and in a very few minutes the bluffs for half a mile up and down the stream were occupied by mounted Indians. We promptly lost our appetites.

This was disturbing enough, but it became more so when they swarmed down the bluffs and charged our camp, a yelling, screeching, painted, nearly naked line of riders. Some had rifles and pistols, but most of them were armed with the bow. They all rode bareback.

We felt pretty nervous as to the outcome of this visit, but none of the Indians fired on us, and none of us pulled a gun. Their impetuous rush soon brought them directly upon us, and they formed a circle about us. One old warrior with a scarred face dashed up almost to my feet, where he pulled his horse to a sudden stop.

Trying to appear greatly pleased at meeting him, I said, in as strong and cheerful a voice as I could command, *"How, mita kola."* (How, my friend.) He jumped from his horse and looked at me for a few moments. Then I said to him in the Lacota tongue: "I look at you. My heart is glad to see my friends."

He stepped forward and inquired, "What is your Lacota name?" I told him my name, *Wambli cigala* (Little Eagle), given to me by the old chiefs of his people — Red Cloud, American Horse, Little Wound, and Young-Man-Afraid-of-His-Horses.

The old warrior then wanted to know whence we came, and where we were going. I told him of our drive with the cattle to the Indians on the Missouri, and said that we were now on our way back to the Platte to take a herd to the Red Cloud Agency on the White River. Then I said to him, "My Lacota friends have bad hearts, but they must not kill the cowboys who bring the cattle which the Great Father sends them, or the soldiers will come in great numbers and with many big guns, and wipe out the Sioux nation."

He said his people were hungry. I told him we had little food, and would be hungry too before

Trying to appear greatly pleased at meeting him, I said, "How, *mita kola*."

we could get to the Shell River (the North Platte).

Springing upon his pony, the old warrior called out to his people who I was, what our party was doing in the country, and what I had said. Yells of "How! How!" came back from all sides.

Packing our camp outfit on our ponies, we started in to round up our horses and drive them across the river, with the help of every Indian in the band. Their mood had changed. There were many "How's!" exchanged as we parted on the south side of the Niobrara.

I have always felt that if ever I had a call to being used as a pincushion, with arrows for pins, that was it; I think there were others about me who shared the weakness that came over me when the ordeal was past. I blessed my past efforts to pick up a little knowledge of the Sioux speech and sign language, for I felt that it had saved all our scalps. There must have been fully three hundred Indians in the bunch that swooped down so suddenly upon our cowboy band of ten.

XX : BIG GAME

My life as a cow waddie came to an abrupt close one day at the end of a long drive over the old Chisholm Trail. After we had delivered the herd to a buyer — the saddle horses not included — I went to my employer and said, "Mr. Bishop, I want to buy Tejon, the pony I've been riding. I bought him for you at San Antonio for eight dollars."

Mr. Bishop looked at me and said, "Why, that horse will bring thirty or forty dollars up here among these Yankees."

That was all that was needed to send me up in the air. I started to tell him what I thought of white-haired cattle drovers in general. I said I had risked my life for him a hundred times in the past months. I had become attached to the horse, and had taught him several tricks; now he wanted to make an exorbitant profit on the pony when I asked to buy him.

"Now, now, now," he exclaimed, "don't talk

that way, boy. You can have the pony. I'll give him to you."

"No, you won't," I said, and added, in a fit of anger, "I can never look at that pony again without thinking of you. But I'll tell you what you have given me. You've given me my freedom from ever working again with any cattleman on the trail to Texas. I'm through."

With that I caught my old horse Roper, settled all accounts with Mr. Bishop, accepted a job from the buyers of the herd we had just driven north, and rode away. My days as a longhorn cowboy were at an end. A short time at my new job, and I took the trail as a hunter of big game.

I sought out and became a partner of Wild Horse Charlie Alexander, who has already come into this story, in the chapter on Mustangs. I had had for some time the ambition to become a hunter. I still had my Winchester, and I knew how to use it. There was plenty of game in the western wilds, and we were going to try our luck at hunting for the market.

Our beginning venture was to get antelope for the Cheyenne market. The first day I did so well with my rifle that Charlie said, "If you can keep this up, all I'll have to do will be to take the meat and hides to Cheyenne, and sell them." I think I did keep it up, too, for Charlie was kept busy hauling our game to market. We made money. Antelope and deer meat ranged from five to eight cents a pound. Dry hides brought from sixteen to twenty-five cents a pound. We soon made profits enough to enable me to buy a fine Sharps 40–90 target rifle, which cost $125. We moulded and patched our bullets, and loaded our own cartridge shells.

Harry Yale, steward of the Union Pacific Hotel in Cheyenne, helped us to sell all the game we could kill and dress, and Colonel Jones, the manager, became so much interested that he bought game for the hotel from us, and also shipped it to other eating places up and down the line of the railroad.

We took pains to have the game we offered for sale well dressed and clean, something about which many hunters were careless. We also took care in stretching, drying, and baling our hides for the market. This created a greater demand for our products than the other hunters enjoyed. To keep up with it, we had to take in another partner, Billy Martin, who was a skilled hunter, and also a temperate man. It was unusual, among the hunters and trappers of that day, that none of us used either drink or tobacco.

In the game-hunting business I made and saved about ten thousand dollars. Game was so plentiful then that I could not foresee the day when it would come so near to extermination as it is today. I am proud that I was never a hide-hunter, and that I never killed game I could not use. Wanton slaughter of animals is, of course, to be deplored.

The extermination of the big game of the West was not an entirely bad thing, however. With vast herds of buffalo and antelope ranging the plains, the great cattle industry could not have been developed. The killing of the buffalo was in large part a military measure aimed at subjugating the Indians. It did more to start the red men on the white man's road, which they are now obliged to follow, than all the force brought to bear upon them by the United States Army.

In the fall of 1879 Colonel Jones sent a party of English sportsmen to our camp in the Shirley Basin in Wyoming, to give them an opportunity to enjoy some big game shooting, and also to give us a chance to make some extra money. These men proved to be a group of fine young fellows, full of life, and good companions all. When they started back to England about a month later, they were loaded down with trophies, and some enjoyable memories of days spent in the Rockies.

Colonel Jones took an increasing interest in us, and sent many interesting people to our camp for a rest or for hunting. Through these contacts I gradually changed my activities. Guiding sportsmen from all parts of the world, and men engaged in research work, grew to be my business. When later I left Wyoming to live in New Mexico for a time, I had a hunting outfit of a hundred head of saddle, work, and pack horses, wagons, pack outfits, a cook, a steward, and camp tenders, as well as camp equipment of all sorts.

The benefits from these trips were greater, however, than mere cash profit. It was an education to travel in this sort of company. I realized that I had an unusual opportunity, and I took advantage of these associations with men of learning to broaden my knowledge. I met Professors E. D. Cope and O. C. Marsh, two of the world's greatest naturalists, and assisted them in their researches in Wyoming, and later in New Mexico. I was of help also to Professors Hayden and King, who carried forward important scientific work in the West. My partners and I were greatly interested in natural history, and we observed closely the natural phenomena of the country over which we ranged while hunting. Evidences of prehistoric plant and animal life were especially interesting to me. Conversations with these scientists aroused a desire to learn more. I was always on the lookout for fossil material that I might pass on to the specialists to study and classify.

After my hunting trip with the party of Englishmen, I made a trip to Cheyenne, where I met Monte Ward, a great baseball player of the day, who wanted to go on a hunt. My old friend Bergersen, leading gunsmith and gundealer of Cheyenne, also wanted to go. I agreed to guide them both.

Before we started, the express agent at Cheyenne came to me and said, "I'll furnish transportation for your outfit, if you'll ship me a nice saddle of mountain sheep for my Christmas dinner.

I expect friends to have dinner with me, and I want to give them a real treat."

I explained that since it was late in the season, probably the snow had driven all the sheep out of the mountains, but that I would gladly try to get him one.

"That's enough for me," he said. "Now I'm sure of my meat."

But when we reached Elk Mountain and I tried to carry out my promise, I found that sure enough, the sheep had left that part of the mountains, and as I had expected, it was impossible to ship the meat for Christmas dinner to the express agent.

One day, however, I killed a really fat antelope — a barren doe, the choicest of all antelope meat. I dressed it carefully. I removed all antelope hair from the meat, and sawed the legs off short, so that the size of the leg bone would not be a give-away. Then, sacking it, I shipped it to him.

We stayed out for several days, and had a good time. Ward had never killed game before, but on this trip he got several antelope. Each of us had brought along a pair of Norwegian snowshoes (skis), to help us over the snow-covered trails. Bergersen was expert on skis, but poor Ward and I had a hard time managing them.

One day Ward and I worked our way nearly to the top of Elk Mountain on our skis. Neither of us had sufficient confidence in his ability to handle skis to be certain of completing a slide down the mountain to the cabin. Ward declared that he would not try it for the world. But I decided to attempt the slide act, and told him to start ahead down the ridge — that I would soon pass him.

The cabin was in plain view at the end of a straightaway slide from the point where we stood, at the top of a canyon nearly filled with soft snow. Ward started to walk down.

After resting a few minutes, I lashed to my back a saddle of antelope we had killed on our way up the mountain, leaving my rifle and steering pole to be carried in my hands. I summoned my courage, turned my skis toward the cabin, and shoved off. The next second I was rushing downward at a terrific rate.

At the point where I was due to pass Ward, I struck a streak of crust over the snow, my skis crossed in front of me, and I sailed into the air, landing on my head in the snow. My skis served to stop me from complete submersion, but I went my full length down into the soft snow, which was yards deep. I had to climb up my own legs, so to speak, to get out, and I emerged nearly smothered and blind, with my mouth, nose, ears, and eyes filled with snow. My rifle was deep down.

As soon as I recovered my breath and looked around, I saw Ward, rolling over and over on the ridge, shouting with laughter.

That was enough for me: I determined to finish that ride or break my neck. I located my rifle by pawing about in the snow, climbed out, and made a fresh start. This time I just about sat on those skis, and kept them well together. I slid clear to the cabin, in the fastest trip I ever made. Ward arrived much later, and it was my turn to laugh.

When we packed up and started back for Cheyenne, I began to dread meeting the express agent. I had not heard from him since sending him the "mountain sheep." As we stepped from the train, he was the first person I saw. He came running up and gave us all a handshake. I could not broach the subject, but Bergersen boldly asked how he had liked the sheep.

"Boys," he said heartily, "it was just great! My friends all said it was the finest meat they ever tasted." Then he went on to say that people could talk to *him* about elk, antelope, deer meat, and the like, but in *his* estimation, mountain sheep was the best meat on earth, and not to be spoken of in the same breath with any other kind of wild game. "I've lived here a long time," he added, "and eaten all kinds of game, until I can tell by the taste just what it is, but believe me, nothing can compare with that mountain sheep you sent me. I'll always remember it."

This was said with such convincing good will that although we were inwardly convulsed, we did not tell him about the trick we had played, nor try to get him to change his opinion of the qualities of mountain sheep meat.

Late one fall when I was hunting with Billy

Martin in the mountains south of the Shirley Basin, there came an eighteen-inch fall of snow. The game in the mountains seemed to be able to tell when it was wise to seek a lower level so as not to be trapped by deep snows. We could see signs that the game were moving to lower feeding grounds. We prepared to break camp and follow.

A few days before the snowfall we had killed three or four elk higher up in the mountains. We had dressed and quartered them, and hung the meat in trees, to be carried to camp later, when we could return with pack horses. Not wanting to lose this meat, Billy and I now took some pack horses and an extra man, and started through the deep snow up into the mountains. We had great difficulty in breaking a trail to the point where we had left the meat. When we reached it, we found that a bear had been before us and had made a feast of our meat. We had hung the hind quarters on stubs of big pine-tree limbs, so we knew the bear must have been very tall, for he had stood on his hind legs and stripped off the fat and kidneys and shredded the best of the meat. What he had not eaten he had left lying about the ground.

We had had no thought of a bear hunt, for the season had arrived when all bears should have been in their dens, taking their winter sleep. But here was a chance to get the largest bear we had seen sign of in the Shirley Basin country.

Billy and I talked it over, and decided to send our assistant back to camp with what meat the bear had left unspoiled, while we went after the thief. Anticipating a long chase, we carried some of the elk meat along with us.

The big fellow had left a plain trail through the deep soft snow. After we had followed for two hundred yards, it made a sharp turn, doubled back almost to the starting point, and then led off in a different direction. We cut across this bend in the trail, and followed along for another hundred yards, until we came to a big pine log over which I could see that the bear had climbed. Mounting the log, I was startled to find that the trail came to an end!

Six feet ahead was a group of young small pines, and by peering hard into them, I could make out a big hairy mass. Bruin was taking a nap; probably the feast he had made of our meat had made him dopey.

His awakening was rude. Billy was right behind me as I crossed the log. When I saw that things were due to happen, I made sign to him to look out. Then I took aim for the middle of that big ball of hair, pulled the trigger of my rifle, and jumped off the log backward.

The next instant I saw and heard things. The great head and shoulders of a huge grizzly loomed up from the other side of that log. I had known that a bear could utter screams, but when he rose up out of his bed in the pines to avenge himself, he made the most fearsome sounds I ever heard. At that short range he looked very tall and wide to me, and much too close; his expression was terrifying.

No sooner did the bear expose his head and body when Billy sent a bullet through his heart. This was too much lead, and he dropped.

The man with the pack animals heard the shots, and came running. We took our bear to camp. In dressing him, we discovered that our bullets had passed through him, not half an inch apart. We shipped the hide and carcass to Cheyenne. One of our customers who owned a meat market sold both meat and hide for us. The hide brought $50; it was an exceptionally large specimen of silver-tip grizzly, in good condition. It remained on exhibition in Cheyenne for some time.

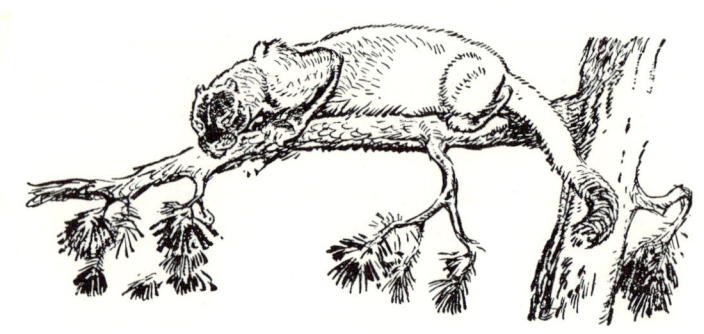

XXI : HUNTER'S LUCK

One night, after a long day of hunting with a number of Englishmen, we returned to camp late, and after getting supper and attending to our stock, it was very dark before I was free to go to the smokehouse, to arrange the fires.

A large number of bones accumulated where we dried and smoked the meat in our camps, and some meat remained on the bones. Naturally, meat-eating animals were drawn to our bone-piles.

Knowing that I might encounter one of the more dangerous animals in the darkness even a short distance from camp, I went well prepared to protect myself. We had no lantern in camp that night, and I took along, to kindle the fire, a bunch of dry grass that I had been using, stuffed into a flour sack, for a pillow.

Kneeling in front of the pit at the smokehouse, I struck a match and set fire to a handful of grass, to give me light to feed the fire. The sudden flare lighted up the surroundings, and as the flame leaped up, something else near by did too, and bounded into the darkness. I was prepared, and took a snap shot at the thing as it disappeared with a growl.

My light died out. I could hear some very unpleasant familiar sounds from a short distance, showing that an animal was wrought up. Blinded by the light, I nevertheless wanted more light — and right away, too. Holding my knife in one hand, I groped about for more dry grass, struck a match, and started a fresh blaze, to which I added fuel.

The men in camp heard my shot and came to my aid, damaging their skin and clothing on the way, for they were unable to find the trail. They wanted to make torches and go right out after the beast, but I vetoed this, for I figured that we had a good-sized cat to deal with, and wounded, at that.

The next morning we marched up the canyon in open formation, in search of traces of last night's prowler. We found him dead just a few feet away from the smokehouse — a puma, big, but very thin, and showing signs of having been in a fight. My shot had struck him in the flank, but had ranged forward and torn the lobe of one lung. I kept his hide for some time.

Even elk hunting, during the days when large bands roamed the mountain ranges of Wyoming, had its dangers. A buck of any one of the deer families, when wounded, could be a desperate warrior. A wounded bull elk might turn on the hunter and do him great injury, especially if its horns were grown, and in fighting condition. I took few chances when dealing with wounded animals, but on one or two occasions I had exciting experiences with them.

One day Billy Martin and I shot down six elk in the pine timber of a mountain south of old Fort Casper. One bull with unusually large horns dropped so suddenly that we thought a bullet had broken his neck. Leaning our rifles against a tree some twenty feet away, we prepared to dress the game. For a few moments I sharpened my knife on my whetstone.

I had picked up a foreleg of the bull, to give my knife a few finishing strops on his hoof — a trick I had learned from Mexicans — when he drew a deep breath and started to his feet. He had been merely creased, and though stunned, he was really unharmed.

I hung on to his foreleg, holding it up so that he could not get his forefeet under him. In some way he succeeded in giving me a kick on the elbow, causing me to lose my hold, and I fell across his neck. Grabbing the horn farthest from the ground, I managed to scramble over and get my feet on his other horn, hoping to be able to hold his head to the ground.

While I was having my troubles at the front, Billy had rushed in to get a hold on the bull's flank, trusting that he might hold him down until I could draw my knife across his throat. The kick on my elbow had driven my knife out of reach, but Billy had not noticed it. Then the bull got his hind legs into action, and Billy, according to his story, was kicked fifteen feet, landing on his back, close to the guns. He scrambled to his feet, grabbed his rifle, and, taking advantage of a moment when he could shoot without hitting me, he ended the fight.

This was my only attempt at bulldogging an elk, and I was glad when it was over. I had a bloody nose and a black eye to care for, the result of whacks on the head from the prongs of the elk's horns. My clothes were stripped nearly off, and I had lost some skin. I should like to see a movie of that scrap, in order to judge whether the elk or the hunter was more scared.

I never killed game that I could not use, but there was one occasion which I regret. We were riding along the Bozeman Trail one hot afternoon when a bunch of ten buffalo straggled into view from behind a butte in front of us, and about a hundred yards away. I was riding one of the best and fastest horses I ever had, a trained hunter, who was ready for action the instant he sighted the buffalo. On an impulse, I let him have his head, and we headed at once for the quarry.

I was soon within range, and drew my rifle. Before my blood cooled, and I realized what I was up to, I had shot down six buffalo. We had no use for meat or hides, as we had plenty of antelope meat on our pack horses, and buffalo hides were useless on a scouting trip. I returned, shamefaced, to my companions, who had halted to watch, and I condemned my own action with the remark that I had sure done a fool stunt. I think they agreed with me.

Leaving the game where it had fallen, we started off again. We had gone a few miles when we met a train of fifteen emigrant wagons, drawn by good horses and mules. The usual dogs gave us our first greeting. As we approached the leading wagon, the train came to a halt, and several men climbed down to talk to us. An old man with long, silver-white hair and beard, who appeared to be the leader, addressed us. He asked the usual questions — "Where are you from?" "Where are you bound?" We answered truthfully and fully. Then he told us that they came out of Arkansas and Missouri, and were headed for the Northwest.

One man in the train seemed overcome by sorrow, as if borne down with great trouble. Moans came from him, although he appeared to be rugged, and of strong spirit. The leader explained that in the night a child had been born to his wife, and the mother had died. They had only that morning laid her in a grave at the side of the trail.

We were told that the party was suffering from lack of water. Little children in many of the wagons were crying for a drink. The train lacked meat, as well; they had seen little game since leaving the Platte River, and had been unable to shoot any, although they had been assured that they would find game along the trail.

I offered to lead them to a good camping spot two miles away, where they would find water and good grazing. I told them of the buffalo I had shot back on the trail, and offered to fill one of their wagons with meat to last out the journey. I agreed to show them how to jerk the meat so that it would not spoil.

We could see that the emigrants, though tempted, were a bit suspicious, and I could understand how they might be, for we were well armed, and our clothing and skin were considerably travel-stained. Possibly they thought we coveted their horses. The men drew aside and held council.

They decided to follow us, probably because they outnumbered us and were also armed, but mostly because they badly needed relief. Thereupon we led the train to a spring of good water. One of the wagons was unloaded, and half a dozen men started with me toward the spot where I had killed the buffalo, leaving my friends in camp with the train.

The men who accompanied me were relieved and delighted when they saw the dead buffalo. The bodies were still warm, and the men could see for themselves that I had told the truth. Their wagon was loaded so full for the return trip that the driver had to walk.

All the party turned out to see the arrival; none of them had ever before seen a buffalo, or eaten its meat. It was a simple meal we had that night, but that feast of broiled steaks was enjoyed as much by those hungry people as a course dinner might have been.

Whatever suspicions may have been directed toward us were now melted in the crucible of good will, and we were invited to stay in camp all night. Possibly they were more content to watch our movements close at hand, within the circle of their night guard, than to have us outside, where they could not see us. At any rate, we made our sleep with them, under the guns of their guard.

The smaller children were put to bed, with full tummies, rather early. Before the elders turned in, the party was assembled and told by the leader that he considered their meeting with us an act of Divine Providence, and that it must have been God's plan that I should kill those buffalo. Perhaps it was; at any rate, I was glad that the only time I acted in violation of my principles of conservation, others benefited. The leader offered up a simple prayer which manifestly came from his heart, thanking God for His kindness to them in their need.

The following morning I showed our new friends how to jerk meat, and then, wishing them a safe journey, we departed, with their blessings following us.

XXII : APACHE OUTBREAK

In the fall of 1882 I went to New Mexico with the Englishmen whom I had guided each year on hunting trips, and helped them to buy large ranches in the southwestern part of the state. I became manager of the W S Ranch, belonging to one of my friends, about eighty miles northwest of Silver City. The other ranches were within fifty miles of the W S, and I helped in their management while I remained in New Mexico.

It was a murderous country in which we set out to conduct a peaceful business. Long before the coming of the whites, this section had been the home of the Apaches, the most warlike and merciless savages with whom the people of the United States have had to deal in winning the West. Proof of their savagery could still be found; skeletons of white men, bearing the marks of bullets, knives, or arrows, and buttons and buckles, and even rotted bits of clothing, often gave evidence of violence and sudden death.

This country had been the stronghold of the old Apache chiefs — of Mangus Colorado, Cochise, Victorio. After the killing of Victorio a short while before we came, there was a lull in Indian warfare, until the summer of 1885. Then came the Geronimo outbreak.

My work on the ranches of my friends made me familiar with all the country between the Mogollon Range and the Arizona and Mexico boundaries. This knowledge was indispensable to me, and helpful to others, during the uprising.

One day an Englishman, Mr. Lyon, who had been visiting some of my friends on the S U ranch, thirty miles north of the W S, came to call on me. He had ridden down several times previously, but this time he came to say good-bye, as he was planning soon to start back to England. The day before his visit ended, we hunted quail all day, and in the morning he started back for the S U. That was the last time I saw him alive.

About half an hour after Lyon left, a man rode up to the W S at full speed, and shouted, incoherently, something about being chased by Indians. He finally made me understand that that morning, while he and some others were camped ten miles west of us, a large party of Indians had attacked their camp, and killed his companions. He had been bringing in the horses, and as he was mounted, he was able to make his escape.

I told him to ride to Alma, a small mining settlement a mile and a half away, to warn the people.

All our cowboys were out on the range, branding calves. Charlie Moore, an old hand who took care of the horses; a Mexican boy; a housekeeper; and I were all that were at the ranch that day. I rushed into the house and warned the housekeeper and the boy. We went to the storeroom for empty gunny sacks, filled them with sand, and piled them in the deep windows of the adobe house, leaving loopholes from which to fire. We opened cases of cartridges and placed them near the arms they were made for.

Charlie Moore came in then, and when he was told about the Indian scare he said that he had just come from the region where the Indians were said to have surrounded the small party, and had seen no Indian sign. It was his opinion that the bearer of the news was drunk or crazy, or both. I decided that in any case, we would get in as many of our saddle horses as we could, and guard them until we knew the truth.

We brought in as many horses as we could get into the corral near the bunkhouse. While we were doing this, five men from Alma came to the ranch to get me to go out on the range with them to find out whether there were any Indians near by. They went on without me, for the people of the Alma and Cooney mining camps were greatly alarmed at the rumor of an Apache uprising, and naturally, they were anxious to know the truth.

As Charlie and I were corraling the horses, one that had been ridden by a member of the party from Alma came to the corral, saddled and bridled; and when we caught him, we knew beyond doubt that the Apaches were on the warpath, for both horse and saddle were bloody. Later, we learned that the men were ambushed only a few miles from the ranch, and two were instantly killed. The rest escaped among the brush and rocks.

I had two teams in a pasture near the house, and sent Moore for them. I rode up on a little hill near the house, where I could overlook the pasture and get a shot at anyone who tried to stop Moore from bringing in the horses. He had gone only a short distance into the pasture when I saw a string of Indians moving toward the horses. Moore couldn't see them, and he was riding in their direction. I shouted to him, but he didn't hear, and then I fired my rifle, checking the Indians for the moment, and causing them to run for cover in the rocks and brush. My horses stampeded when the savages returned my fire, and came running to their stable, safe.

Moore located the Apaches by their shooting, and got to high ground, from which he could see them. He added a few shots to mine, and the Indians made a run for it. With so great a range, and such rapidly-moving targets, our bullets were ineffective.

Night was coming, and Charlie and I went back to the house. We stood guard all night, he at the corrals, I at the ranch house. I took my revolvers and two double-barreled shotguns, and stayed outside within the shadow of the buildings. As day broke, the housekeeper called to me to come in and get my coffee.

In the time it took me to drink a cup, we had Indian visitors. When I returned to my station by a storehouse a few feet from the kitchen door, I found that two Apaches had approached the storehouse. I studied their tracks. One savage wore moccasins; the other was barefoot.

I was startled, but by following their tracks in the soft earth, I saw that they had gone. I signaled to Charlie to come to me, and we trailed the Indians. It was daylight, and we followed the trail to the top of a hill near the ranch, where we found that our visitors had been joined by others. With field glasses, I studied the trails leading into the Mogollon Mountains; and along the Deep Creek Trail I made out a line of moving animals or human beings. They were too far away for me to identify them, but as no range stock had ever traveled that trail, I was sure they were Indians.

We returned to the ranch. After getting breakfast, Charlie and I rode to the top of a hill, where we could overlook our horse range. We left our horses hidden in a clump of trees and climbed to a place among the rocks where we could get a good view of the countryside with our glasses. I detected movement along the Eagle Creek Trail, which led within a hundred yards of our hiding-place. The objects were coming toward us, and as they came still nearer I could make out a dozen Indians on foot, and a white man, mounted on a mule, behind them.

Charlie said, "Let's let them come right up to us, and kill the whole outfit before they can get to cover."

I told him not to fire until I did. By this time they were a hundred yards away. Letting them get still closer, I called out, "Halt! Don't try to run!"

The man on the mule pulled up, and the Indians, after a word from him, kept still.

"Who are you?" I demanded.

"Lieutenant Gatewood, and these men are scouts," was the answer.

I rose up in full view and ordered the Lieutenant to approach. He came within thirty yards, and asked me who I was. When I told him, he wanted to know if I were the hunter and guide, Jim Cook, of whom he had heard Captain Emmet Crawford speak. I said I probably was, inasmuch as Captain Crawford was a friend of mine.

Greetings followed, and then Gatewood told me that he had been stationed at Camp Apache in command of a company of Indian scouts; that Geronimo and his band had broken away from their reservation, where they had been held as prisoners; and that he had got together a few of his scouts and started in pursuit. He was being followed by a pack train and two troops of the Fourth U. S. Cavalry, commanded by Captain

Allen Smith and Lieutenant Parker. Looking back along Eagle Creek Trail, I could see the troops coming, even as he spoke. Gatewood said he and the troops had left the trail of the Indians a short distance back, and were rushing for the San Francisco River to give the command a chance to get food and water. I told him where he could make a cut-off and strike the main trail of the Indians over at Deep Creek.

When the troops came up, we all went back to the ranch, where they had breakfast and an hour's rest. Captain Smith told of burying the bodies of a number of victims of the uprising. We were heavy-hearted at the prospect of murder and plundering and destruction that must follow before the Apaches could be subdued.

While the troops were at breakfast, a messenger came in from Alma with word of the ambush of the day before, and wanted me to help in the search for the bodies of two of the scouting party. Since the direction they had taken was in the line of march of the troops, which were to strike the Indian trail at Deep Creek, I asked the Captain to help. He agreed, and I went with the command, with the double purpose of finding the massacred men and of guiding the troops to Deep Creek.

We located the bodies without any trouble; they lay near the trail. I left them for a time, and led the troops to the point on the Deep Creek Trail where I had that morning seen movement. It was the trail of the main body of Indians, and the troops lost no time in starting off in the direction taken by the enemy.

At this point I turned back, got some men from Alma, and led them to the point where the bodies of their comrades lay. They put them upon horses, and carried them home for burial.

Something had been bothering me. The trail of the Indians led in the direction of Devil's Park, a place in the mountains named by gold prospectors because of its secret situation. A man named Stallworth lived there with his family in a log cabin. Charlie Moore and I now spurred our horses toward the Stallworths', with the same thought in our minds.

From a point near the cabin we first heard rapid firing, and knew that an attack was being made on the family. Leaving our horses concealed in a thicket, we hurried to our neighbors' aid.

Two of Geronimo's warriors died when we opened fire. The rest, about a dozen, hastily departed into the rough shelter of gulches and timber, firing a few shots in defiance as they ran. Possibly if they had known the size of the rescue party, the incident might have ended disastrously for us; but the firing ended and the attackers left, probably to hunt for other victims less well defended.

Mr. Stallworth came out of the cabin with his family, and after caring for Mrs. Stallworth, who was wounded, we heard their story.

Just before we came, Mrs. Stallworth was on

the doorstep, giving her children their lessons. Looking up, she saw an Indian, rifle in hand, stealthily zig-zagging from tree to tree near the house. She pulled the children into the house. She closed and barred the door, just as a bullet crashed through the planks and tore through her arm.

Inside, Mr. Stallworth was mending a saddle. He was a good shot, and he had a rifle, but he had only two or three cartridges. These he did not want to use except as a last resort. He took one cartridge which had missed fire the first time he used it, and fired at an Indian near the house, but again it failed to explode. We had surely come just in time.

I sent Charlie to Alma to get help to take this family to a safe place, and I stayed with them until help came. It seemed likely that there might be a second attack at any moment. It was seldom that Indians left the bodies of their fellow warriors unburied. No attempt to get their bodies was made, though, and even days later, when Stallworth returned to his cabin, he found that the only visitors had been animals and buzzards which left but little of the bodies for him to dispose of.

I left when the relief party arrived, and followed the trail of Geronimo's band. I soon met Lieutenant Gatewood and some of his Apache scouts, who were leading the troops back over a trail they had been following. The rear guard of the Indians had concealed themselves on a bluff which

Geronimo's rear guard had concealed themselves on a bluff which could not be scaled by troops, and fired into the command.

could not be scaled by troops, and had fired into them as they halted for a ten-minute rest, killing several horses, and wounding a scout. After this attack they had fled toward Fort Bayard and Silver City, eighty miles away. Their trail led into the roughest part of the Mogollon range; between the command and Fort Bayard lay the Gila River canyon, which could not be crossed by mounted men for many miles above or below, although Indians on foot could cross it by scaling the precipices. It was the custom of the Apaches, when pursued, to head for the most inaccessible parts of the mountains. If they were mounted, they would ride as far as their horses could go, then kill them and scatter like quail, to meet at some prearranged spot later on.

Captain Smith's command had exhausted the supplies necessary for horses and men, and had to turn back. It was at this point that I came upon them. The Captain was anxious to get a message to Fort Bayard, hoping that the troops there might be able to intercept the Indians. As there was no one in his command who knew the trails to Fort Bayard, and as their horses were unfit for such work, I volunteered to carry the message.

In order to save time I selected an indirect route, following roads and trails over fairly open country for one hundred and ten miles or more. I left at five that afternoon. I had the use of mail horses from the Mormon settlement on the San Francisco River to Silver City, and from Silver

City to the fort I rode a livery horse. The night was cloudy, and all objects were indistinct. I certainly *thought* I saw a lot of Indians on that ride. Bits of soapweed and dead stumps looked alive to me. But I got through, and at sunrise I was within the fort.

Sixteen persons died that night at the hands of the Apaches on the trail between Devil's Park and Fort Bayard. That morning shortly after sunrise they murdered a number of people within three miles of the fort.

Soon the Sixth Cavalry troopers were out scouring the country for Indians. (The keen pursuit of this expedition eventually forced the main body of Geronimo's band to scatter and escape for a time to Mexico.)

I was anxious to get back to the ranch, and after receiving an answer to the message I had carried, I started back, arriving at the ranch by midnight. I stopped off at the camp long enough to deliver the message to Captain Smith.

Arriving at the W S, I found that my outfit had returned. The Indians had passed within two miles of them. Working down Blue Creek, the boys had struck Indian sign in the form of moccasin tracks, and of horses lanced to death. They found the bodies of three prospectors; one of them had been caught away from camp without arms, and been beaten to death with rocks.

Some of my friends from the S U Ranch were waiting for me. Mr. Lyon had not returned to the S U after leaving me, and they feared he was dead. At four o'clock that morning we went out to search for Lyon. We found his body near the trail. His horse and saddle were gone. The sign indicated that he had been reading a letter from home while riding along. The Apaches had ambushed him, letting him come within ten feet. The shot that killed him tore a great hole in his body, and knocked him from his horse. The savages did not delay to mutilate his body, but took his gun and cartridge belt. After they had gone Lyon apparently had recovered sufficiently to get to his feet and stagger a little way. He had rolled up his shirt above the wound, fallen again, and died. Sadly, we carried him back to the ranch and buried him.

XXIII : GERONIMO'S TRAIL

Troops from Fort Bayard soon were stationed at Alma, and two troops of the 8th Cavalry made their headquarters at the W S until the end of the campaign. I scouted for them whenever small bands of Indians came within striking reach.

On one of these trips Major Sumner, in command of one of the troops, was ordered to a point about fifty miles from the W S, in the mountains along the Gila River, to pick up an Indian trail lost by a company of militia. I went with them, and we reached the place quickly, found the trail, and followed it until nightfall. Just at dusk, a courier arrived to inform us that a freighter had been killed by Indians that morning near the White House Ranch, on the road between Alma and Silver City.

The trail we had been following was several days old. Since it seemed likely that the savages we were trailing were the same band that had killed the freighter, Major Sumner decided to try to pick up a fresh trail at the scene of the murder. It was over twenty miles to the spot, but we moved there before daylight, and the command was hidden in a gulch near the ranch; Indians kept a constant watch for troops, and great caution was necessary.

After a short rest I went out with a new guide, who was supposed to have a thorough knowledge of the Mogollon range, having prospected and hunted there for years. We went to the place where the freighter had been ambushed. I identified him as Sauborin, a man I had known, who owned a general store in the Cooney mining camp. As the freighters who usually hauled his supplies would not risk it during the Indian uprising, Sauborin had taken his own team, and was on his way back from Silver City with a load of goods when the Apaches had riddled him with bullets. His team had run away with the load, and been caught about a mile farther on. What the Indians couldn't carry away from the wagon, they destroyed.

We followed the trail for about ten miles into the mountains. Serious though it was, trailing this band had its comical side. The Apaches had left a plain trail. They had carried away from Sauborin's wagon a quantity of candy. What did not suit their taste, such as "heart mottoes," they discarded. I picked up a number of these heart candies; they bore such messages as "I Love You"; "Kiss Me"; "You Are My Honey." A box of fancy perfumed toilet soap, mistaken for candy, had been carried along, until the bearer tasted it. One cake showed a row of deep tooth marks on each side, and a dent in the cake told of the disgust with which it had been hurled from a red hand.

We returned to the troop, and when it was dark the command moved to the point where we had left the trail, and there we rested until daylight. This country was so rough that I could not ride my horse, and he was put into the pack train. The cavalry horses had to be led.

When we left Duck Creek near the White House Ranch, we knew that the trail was leading into a country where there was no water for many miles. Canteens were ordered filled, and all were cautioned to use water sparingly. With no canteen, I expected to make a dry trip.

We followed the trail all that hot day, deep into the mountains. It was hard climbing. When night came, and we could no longer make out the trail, we lay down. Horses and men were now suffering for water. We had hard bread and bacon to eat. One man complained loudly because he was forbidden to make a cup of coffee. His voice was disturbing, and could be heard a long distance in the quiet mountains.

At last Major Sumner called one of his officers to him. "Tell that man he's making as much noise as if he were drawing a general's pay, and that I would like to have him keep as quiet as possible for a few hours." The man subsided.

We could tell from the sign that we were close to the Indians, and the next morning I went with the other guide and a small detachment to try to find the Indian camp. Before we had gone three miles we found it; but the alert redskins must have heard our thirsty horses whinnering and braying during the night, for they had killed their horses, smothered the fires on which they had been roasting meat, and fled.

The soldiers returned to the command, and we two guides separated, each to try to trail an Indian to the meeting place we were sure they had appointed; once they banded together again, they would make a trail that the troops could follow swiftly. It was arranged that the troops would move up to the deserted camp to wait for us.

I had followed a trail for perhaps a half-mile when I heard a shot from the direction taken by the other guide, and thought he had been ambushed by Indians. There was nothing I could do to save him, but I decided to return to camp, by way of the spot where I had heard the shot fired. I was extremely tired and thirsty, and the trail seemed to lead straight for the Gila Canyon, which no horse could cross for forty miles.

It was hard going, and out of my way, but I struck his trail, to find that it led back toward the camp which had been deserted by the Indians. I followed it straight to the troops. There I found the guide, alive, and apparently unharmed. When I asked him what he had fired at, he told me he had spotted a big buck deer, and that he had shot at it before he thought. His service with the command ended that day.

While I was telling the man what I thought of him, Major Sumner came up to me and said, "Jim, will you have a drink?" I said, "No, thanks, Major, I had a drink last week."

But as he placed his canteen in my hand I discovered by its weight that it was full. My tongue was thick, and I was burningly thirsty. In his quiet way, the Major explained, "Jim, in this life, men sometimes get hurt, and need water badly." I told him that in appreciation of his unselfishness, I would take a wee drop.

As the water in his canteen was probably all there was in the whole command, and as he was having to walk, and lead his horse, just as everyone else did, that act made a deep impression on my mind. I had been able to pay scant attention to what was going on back there with the troop. Doubtless the other officers and Dr. Maddox had shared the water in their canteens with some of the weaker troopers. There are always men who will not or cannot stand hardships.

Our next imperative need was to get to water. Mogollon Creek, twenty miles away, was nearest, and we started toward it. A cloudburst drenched us before we reached it, and when we got there I spied some W S cattle. It was not long before we were eating fresh beef. Since the storm had washed away the trail, we returned to the ranch.

Along toward the end of the campaign, we received word that Geronimo and his band were across the border in Mexico. Having been under a terrific strain for a long time, I decided to get a few days' rest, and went to visit friends at Camp Carlin and at Fort D. A. Russell, in Wyoming.

I had scarcely arrived when a message came, telling of the ambush of C Troop of the 8th Cavalry while on its way from the W S Ranch to Silver City for supplies.

Lieutenant Fountain, in command of C Troop, had some Navajo scouts who, like many scouts used in campaigns in the Southwest, seemed extraordinarily well informed of the movements of the hostiles being pursued. How they managed to keep in such close touch with the enemy was not clear, but it was a fact that whenever danger was imminent, they would either balk outright, or have to stop to "make medicine" until the crisis was past.

This time the scouts were slow in breaking camp and taking their positions ahead of the command. Lieutenant Fountain started the troop and wagons on the road, and then went back to the scouts, to hurry them up. Before he could return to his men, the Apaches fired into them at close range.

Dr. Maddox was the first man hit. The bullet that struck him did not knock him from his horse, although it made a mortal wound. He dismounted and, turning to a trooper near him, said,

"Babcock, don't bother about me — save yourself; I shall be dead in a minute." Just then another bullet struck him, and he fell dead. The Doctor was a man beloved by all.

Among the victims was a trooper named Wishart, one of the strongest men in the 8th Cavalry. His back was broken by a bullet, and he lived just a little while after the Indians were routed, then died in Lieutenant Fountain's arms. A number of others were killed and wounded.

Department headquarters had evidently been misinformed as to the whereabouts of Geronimo.

Some sad or unusual things happened during the Geronimo uprising. When the news first reached Alma, all the people in the settlement except George Herr and his wife helped to fortify a large adobe store building in the center of the settlement, into which they moved for protection. The Herrs piled a lot of sacks filled with sand into the windows of their little adobe house, and said they would take their chances there.

The first night, Mr. Herr went to bed with a revolver under his pillow. As he got out of bed in the morning, the revolver dropped to the floor, and struck on the hammer, exploding the cartridge. The bullet struck him in the head, and killed him instantly.

A cowboy from the old White House Ranch on Duck Creek was out on the range looking for some horses one day, when, going up the side of a steep foothill, he rode right into an ambush.

The Indians opened fire on him at short range, but missed him and his horse, too. The firing frightened the horse — one of the hair-trigger variety of broncho — and it promptly tucked its head down between its legs and gave those Indians a splendid exhibition of a horse bucking down the side of a mountain, over boulders, shrubs, trees, and all other obstacles.

The Indians must have been entertained, for they forgot to shoot until horse and rider were away, and making tracks for the home ranch. Then they began firing occasional shots at him as he fanned his broncho along with his quirt. When he had gone half a mile or more, a chance bullet struck him in the back of the neck; but instead of breaking his neck or cutting the jugular vein, as might be expected, it passed through the flesh without knocking him from his horse or doing him any serious injury. That cowboy certainly had "good luck that shot."

The man who deserved the greatest credit for the capture of Geronimo and his band was Lieutenant Gatewood. Had it not been for his heroic work, Geronimo would probably have been out for some time longer, and many more would have lost their lives at the hands of his warriors. Gatewood knew Geronimo, and spoke his language to a certain extent. Geronimo knew that Gatewood's tongue was not forked, and trusted him well enough to follow his advice.

But Gatewood surely put his life in chancery

when he went, alone, into Geronimo's camp down in Mexico, to persuade this last of the bloodthirsty old Apache war chiefs to surrender himself and his people, with no other promises made him than that they would be protected from vengeance at the hands of the white settlers. Geronimo's faith in Gatewood must have been strong, for he had time to change his mind before he and his people reached Captain Lawton's camp, north of the boundary line, and surrendered. If he had known that he and his warriors were to be exiled to far-off Florida, never again to see the land of their forefathers, I think the wily old chief would have preferred death in the land of his birth.

Without question, Geronimo will receive attention from historians; but I hope that the name of the brave lieutenant who underwent such hardships and desperate risks to capture the clever, dangerous old chief will receive honorable mention in the record of the final deeds of Geronimo's fighting days.

XXIV : HOME ON THE RANGE

In 1879, when I was in Cheyenne, I had met pioneer Dr. E. B. Graham and his family. In 1879 the doctor had established one of the first two cattle ranches in the upper Niobrara Valley, in Nebraska, about a hundred and fifty miles northeast of Cheyenne. The Grahams lived in Cheyenne during the greater part of the year, while hired men took care of the ranch and herd.

Having more than a casual interest in the younger daughter, I had contrived to look in at the ranch more than once when the family was vacationing there; the horseback trip of three or four hundred miles meant little to me, when I could see my girl at the end of the trip.

Soon after the close of the Geronimo campaign I went back to Cheyenne, and when I returned to the W S Ranch in the autumn of 1886, I brought Kate Graham with me as my wife. We lived at the W S for a brief time after our marriage, and then I sold my interest in the ranch, and we moved to Cheyenne.

The year following our marriage I bought from my father-in-law his cattle and ranch in the Niobrara Valley. The O 4 Ranch became the Agate Springs Ranch, and ever since then it has been our home.

The days of the open range and the roundup system came to a close in Nebraska soon after we established ourselves at the old ranch. Home seekers and builders came in to possess the range which cattlemen had been accustomed to use freely; from that time on, they had to buy or lease their grazing lands. Wire fences, windmills, cabins of log and sod and lumber, soon were erected on the most desirable of the old grazing grounds of the state. The flocks of antelope, the white-tailed and mule-eared deer, began to vanish before the advancing settlers.

There seemed little reason for those who settled in northwestern Nebraska after the middle eighties to fear Indians. Nevertheless, the unexpected did occur. During the winter of 1890–91, while I was busy developing my ranch, there was a genuine Indian scare — the Ghost Dance War,[1] as it was named by the Sioux.

As this widespread war, brought on by the Messiah craze, neared its end, a band of Sioux under

[1] A publication of the Bureau of Ethnology of the Smithsonian Institute at Washington, D. C., gives a truthful and complete account of this uprising, which it terms the "Sioux Outbreak of 1890," and describes the trouble caused by the Messiah craze which swept all the Indian reservations of the West, and resulted in the death of three hundred Indian men, women, and children, and thirty-one soldiers, on December 29, 1890.

Chief Big Foot left the Standing Rock Reservation for the Pine Ridge Reservation, South Dakota, to surrender to the soldiers. When it became known where the surrender was to take place, a number of civilians at the Agency prepared to be on hand to see Big Foot and his people give themselves up. There were newspapermen from a number of newspapers, including one European correspondent.

I went to the Reservation in response to urgent messages, shipping my horse and riding the same train to Rushville, whence I rode to Pine Ridge. Since I was requested to work with the quartermaster scouts, I had no further use for my horse, and foolishly lent him to a newspaperman who wanted to get to Wounded Knee Creek, where the surrender was to take place.

When the reporter reached the vicinity of Wounded Knee Creek, he turned my horse over to another man, who rode him directly to the scene of the coming surrender. There he dismounted, threw the reins to the ground, and left the horse to take care of himself.

Big Foot's band arrived, and his braves were directed to bring out their arms and get in line. They did so. Just when all was ready, and they were about to permit themselves to be disarmed by the soldiers, an old medicine man in line leaned over, picked up a handful of dirt, and threw it up into the air, making the sign, "back to the earth," and shouting, "They are going to kill us!"

That was the needed spark. A young Indian dropped his blanket from his shoulders and fired at the nearest soldier. The battle was on. The soldiers returned the fire, and machine guns helped to mow down the frenzied red men. In a few minutes the snow was bright red with the blood of several hundred of them.

When that gruesome, unnecessary slaughter was over, the man who had borrowed my horse looked for him, and not finding him where he had left him, concluded that he had run away; but as he glanced around, he discovered my horse, standing behind a machine gun that had been in operation. A bullet had cut a flesh wound a foot long in his shoulder, but he had stood his ground throughout that bloody fight. He had been trained to stand when the reins were on the ground, and he did.

That the Wounded Knee tragedy could take place without retaliation from the Indians, was due only to the red men's being divided among themselves. The influences of civilization were at work. Many saw the futility of further losing wars with the whites. Father was arrayed against son; brother, against brother. The season of the year was against a general outbreak, and by the time of the new green grass, their fighting blood had cooled.

During the years following the Wounded Knee disaster, Chief Red Cloud visited me a number of times, accompanied by his people, seventy or more in number. The last visit he paid me was in 1908, when he stayed ten days, and told me many stories of his efforts to stop the whites from passing through his country, and of his fights with the Pawnees, Crows, and other tribes. Each year, he and his people brought me gifts of Indian relics, some of them dating back to the time when a man with a white skin was as scarce in Sioux country as a white beaver.

There was another side to Red Cloud besides that of the villainous murderer and horse thief that he has been called. The chief visited me early one September, when my eldest son was preparing to leave for school in Lincoln — the first time he had ever been separated from us.

The Indians in their lodges a hundred yards from the ranch house knew that our son was leaving us. When the time came for him to go, the old women, with quiet solemnity, lined up on both sides of the walk leading to the driveway, and as my son passed between them, each woman gave him a handclasp. Then all began to chant the songs they used to sing when they parted from their own kinsmen. My son entered the carriage, and as it passed the Indian lodges, the old men came out, dressed in their best, with old Red Cloud in the lead. The chieftain took my son in his arms and held him close. Placing his cheek against the boy's, and patting his back, he said, "I am an old man. Your father is my friend. I and all my people will give you his name and think of you with good hearts."

All the men came forward then and embraced the boy, whose eyes by this time were wet, as were those of a number of the women, both red and white.

Many people think the Indian lacked a sense of humor, but some that I knew seemed to see the funny side of things. Thirty years ago, a large party of Ogalalla Sioux came over from the Pine Ridge Agency to my ranch for a visit. Among them were Red Cloud and his family, Little Wound, American Horse, No Water, Big Road, He Dog, and other famous warriors, as well as Corn Cob and Black Elk, two prominent medicine men of the tribe.

One of the red men, an old man named Wolf's Ears, I had never seen before. He was among the last to come up and shake my hand when I greeted the party. As I was about to mount my horse and ride away, Wolf's Ears invited me to his tepee, saying that he had something to tell me. I entered his lodge and sat down. The old Indian produced a pipe from his heart bag, filled it with tobacco and the inner bark of dogwood, and made a little smoke.

Then he told me solemnly, in a low voice, that a few years before, he had met a white man friend living in the Black Hills country. Whenever he visited this man, his white friend always killed eight or ten cattle for him and the families that accompanied him on these visits, so that they could have a fine feast of meat.

I said I was glad to know that the Indian had such a good friend, and I asked what had become of him.

"He is dead," said Wolf's Ears, sadly.

"But what killed him?" I inquired.

"I do not know," answered the old Indian.

"Well," I said, with as straight a face as I could command. "I will tell you what killed him. Giving eight or ten cattle to an Indian would kill any white man. I shall be sure not to do such a thing, now that you have told me what happened to your friend."

Wolf's Ears saw the point, and he broke into a hearty laugh. I said "Wa-ga-nisk-ta," ("I am going now"), and left him. I could hear him laughing mightily, even when I had gone a hundred feet from his tepee.

When Red Cloud was born, the West was a vast wilderness. When he was old enough to join the hunters and warriors, the whites had scarcely begun to explore the western wilds. His eyes had grown dim with age before the white man had accomplished the complete subjugation of his people. His right as a ruler to oppose the oncoming paleface, he never abdicated. He died as he had lived — an Indian who never pretended to be reconstructed.

Some of the young Indians have now advanced so far that they are almost ashamed of their old fathers and mothers, and of their primitive habits. They should instead be proud of the many virtues of their people. The red man possessed many qualities that might well be copied not only by his children, but by all of us. He had faults, too, in common with other men; but he left a rich heritage for America.

Until their side of the question has been examined, the old Indians who knew the wild free life of early America should not be condemned by those who occupy their former lodge sites. It was only natural for the Indian to look upon the invasion and conquest of his country with the same feeling that we would today experience if a foreign nation should attempt to invade our country. Although I have been close to death at the hands of Indians, and have seen some dear friends killed by them, I have never, to the amazement of some, regarded the proverbial dead Indian as the only good Indian. I can only say that had I been born with a red skin, I might have been a bad Indian, from the white man's point of view.

It is to be hoped that in all our future dealings with the Indians, whom at first we forced, and now are leading, into our way of life, we will be just and honorable; and that these red people will soon be accorded rights and advantages at least equal to those given to the masses from other parts of the world who come to enjoy the opportunities and protection we offer so freely. Education of the right kind is all that is needed to make good citizens of the Indians.

One day before I was married, while visiting

the Graham ranch on the Niobrara, I made what turned out to be an important discovery. Riding along the picturesque buttes that skirt the river, I came upon two high, conical hills, about three miles from the ranch house. I dismounted, and leaving the reins of my bridle trailing on the ground, I climbed the steep side of one of the hills, from which there was an unobstructed view for miles up and down the valley. I wanted to get a good look at the beautiful country.

About half way to the summit, I noticed fragments of bones scattered over the ground. At first I thought that many years ago some Indian brave might have been laid to his long rest under one of the shelving rocks near the crest of the hill, and a number of his ponies killed, after the custom of certain tribes, to serve him in the Happy Hunting Grounds. But I noted a peculiar glitter on one of the bones, and picking it up, I discovered that it was a beautiful petrified piece of the shaft of some creature's leg bone. The marrow cavity was filled with tiny calcite crystals, enough exposed to cause the glitter that had attracted my attention.

I left my discovery there, but shortly after I took my sweetheart, Kate, to the spot. When we returned to the ranch we carried with us what was doubtless the first fossil material ever taken from the Agate Springs Fossil Quarry.

Later I brought our discovery to the attention of scientists, and in the summer of 1904 Mr. O. C.

Peterson, collector for the Carnegie Institute at Pittsburgh, came at my invitation to prospect for fossils on our ranch. My son Harold and I took him to the conical hills. He had dug only a short time when he uncovered a deposit of petrified bones, leading back into the stone of the hillside.

So valuable were the first specimens that the Institute carried on further excavations, and secured a fine collection of fossils representative of the region. The hills were given the name Agate Springs Fossil Quarry after my ranch, which in turn had been named for the springs that come from the agatized rock near the ranch. One of the two hills was called Carnegie Hill, and the other, University Hill.

Since the first fossil material was taken from the quarry, some of the most distinguished men of the scientific world have visited the place, and many tons of petrified bones of prehistoric animals of the early Miocene period have been collected by paleontologists for the Carnegie Institute, the national museum at Washington, the American Museum of Natural History, and for the museums at Yale, Amherst, Princeton, and many other colleges and cities all over the world.

The evidence shows that back in the Oligocene and early Miocene times, the country around Agate somewhat resembled the mouth of the Amazon — a great flood plain. Animal life fled to high ground to escape being trapped by sudden floods. Often creatures that would not ordinarily have lived together harmoniously were forced together by the flood waters. Then sometimes a still higher rise of water would trap these animals, and their bodies would be carried off and deposited in drifts made by eddies. The deposit of petrified bones at Agate is believed to represent such a drift.

For countless ages the story of the earth has been recorded in the mountains and the valleys, and man is ever engaged in trying to read the record. As a boy I had been interested in nature study. Scientists I met later stimulated my interest and added to my knowledge. My son Harold, a trained paleontologist, has kept me interested. Through important discoveries he made, he has had his name entered into scientific nomenclature. Not far from the ranch he picked up a petrified tooth which has attracted more attention than any other fossil discovery made in the region. If further evidence proves beyond all doubt that this tooth belonged to our immediate ancestor in the human succession, it will carry the life story of mankind back thousands of years into the Lower Pliocene age. In honor of its discoverer, Professor Henry Fairfield Osborn has given to the object the name *Hesperopithicus haroldcookii*.

In this volume I have recorded another, newer story — that of an American boy on our western frontiers, and his experiences with vaqueros, longhorns, and Indians on the cattle trails. It was my fortune to be among the first to work with the wild cattle in the mesquite and the chaparral thickets of pioneer Texas, and on the trails leading from them.

That life near to nature, lacking in excesses and frills, tended to make men. Most of the boys I knew were honest, generous to a fault, respectful to women and to the aged. The sunshine and wind and hard riding of the plains helped, I believe, to develop self-reliant and efficient men. I look with pride back to those old cowboys. They did a good job, whether on the range, in the governor's mansion, or in the presidential chair.

Through moving pictures, and through books and music and painting and sculpture, the cowboy may continue to live for many generations. Some of those cowboys of the wild-longhorn days of the old Chisholm Trail, when not a barbed-wire fence broke the wilderness between Corpus Christi and the Assiniboine near the Canadian line, are now wearing silver in their hair. Most of them have already gone to their last roundup. I hope that those who are still with us, and who may read what I have written, will feel that I have hit at least some of the high ground of truth.